WHAT ARE YOU AFRAID OF?

Being assertive? Looking fat? Speaking in public? Getting older? Going broke? Are you afraid for you children? Afraid of losing love? Afraid of leading the charge?

Women everywhere confront these and many other fears every day.

Enter Arianna Huffington, bestselling author, Internet entrepreneur, journalist, mother, and one of the most influential people in America.

ON BECOMING FEARLESS

... in Love, Work, and Life

"A new book for women about how to defeat their wiliest enemies — fear, phobia, and inhibition. . . . One of the strong suits of *On Becoming Fearless* is its intermittent exploration of various ways of coping with such fears — simple things, or little disciplines to practice."
                                                        — *Elle*

"*On Becoming Fearless* makes you think. . . . This book may encourage readers to prioritize their fears — to do something, perhaps, about what they can change and to accept being scared to death about the rest."
                                                — *Washington Post*

"This may be Huffington's most radicalizing influence as an opinion-maker and role model: the undeniable appeal of someone who is perpetually unafraid of being the tallest girl in the room."   —*New York*

"Huffington's strident voice and populist sympathies make this an encouraging call to arms against the forces that would keep women 'sacrificing our personal truth to go along, be approved of, or just plain be "nice."'"   —*Publishers Weekly*

"Huffington must be the first self-help book author ever to quote Goethe, Shaw, Freud, Nietzsche, and Gandhi and also tout the benefits of microdermabrasions and the liberating effects of menopause."   —*San Francisco Chronicle*

"For such a glamorous and forceful figure, Huffington is hyperaware of the things that hold women back."   —*House & Garden*

"Surprisingly refreshing. . . . A wide-ranging look at the challenges women face in family, faith, careers, and personal fulfillment to explore the rewards of facing up to fears and working steadily toward fearlessness."   —*Booklist*

ON BECOMING
FEARLESS

Also by Arianna Huffington

The Female Woman

After Reason

Maria Callas: The Woman Behind the Legend

The Gods of Greece

Picasso: Creator and Destroyer

The Fourth Instinct: The Call of the Soul

Greetings from the Lincoln Bedroom

How to Overthrow the Government

Pigs at the Trough: How Corporate Greed and Political Corruption Are Undermining America

Fanatics and Fools: The Game Plan for Winning Back America

ON BECOMING
FEARLESS

. . . in Love, Work, and Life

Arianna Huffington

LITTLE, BROWN AND COMPANY

New York | Boston | London

Little, Brown and Company
Hachette Book Group
237 Park Avenue, New York, NY 10017
www.hachettebookgroup.com

Originally published in hardcover by Little, Brown and Company,
    September 2006
First paperback edition, April 2007

Little, Brown and Company is a division of Hachette Book Group, Inc.
The Little, Brown name and logo are trademarks of Hachette Book
Group, Inc.

Library of Congress Cataloging-in-Publication Data
Huffington, Arianna.
    On becoming fearless: a road map for women / Arianna Huffington.—1st ed.
    p. cm.
    ISBN 978-0-316-16681-2 (hc) / 978-0-316-16682-9 (pb)
    1. Women— Psychology.   2. Courage—Miscellanea.   I. Title.
HQ1206.H795   2006
305.42—dc22   2006017005

10   9   8   7   6   5

RRD-IN

Book designed by Paula Russell Szafranski

Printed in the United States of America

*For my mother, Elli, whose fearless spirit
permeates this book.
For my daughters, Christina and Isabella, as they
find their paths to fearlessness.
And for Kenny, my Huffington Post partner,
whose love and support have made my own
journey more fearless.*

$\mathscr{C}$ontents

Contents

ON BECOMING
FEARLESS

Introduction

———◆———

I REMEMBER IN February 1997 taking my then seven- and five-year-old daughters to an exhibition of Shakespeare's "Unruly Women" at the Folger Shakespeare Library in Washington. There was Portia in *The Merchant of Venice,* who takes on the whole Venetian legal world and uses the law to bring new, deeper insights to it. There was Beatrice in *Much Ado About Nothing,* and Rosalind in *As You Like It,* both of them "take no prisoners" women who ruffled the feathers of those birdbrains mindlessly parroting the status quo.

Fearless women come in all shapes, forms, ages, and professions. As Shakespeare put it, "Age cannot wither her, nor custom stale her infinite variety."

I wanted to take my daughters to that exhibition because it's never too early to teach women fearlessness. But now as I watch my girls in their teenage years, I'm stunned to see all the same classic fears I was burdened with: How attractive am I? Do people like me? Should I speak up? I wonder if their fears are more intense than mine were at their age or if they just seem more intense. I had thought that with all the gains feminism has brought, my daughters would not have to suffer through the fears I did. Yet here is our younger generation, as uncertain, doubting, and desperate as we were, trying to fulfill the expectations of others. What happened to our bold little girls?

As Mary Pipher puts it in her bestselling book *Reviving Ophelia: Saving the Selves of Adolescent Girls,* "Something dramatic happens to girls in early adolescence. Just as planes and ships disappear mysteriously into the Bermuda Triangle, so do the selves of girls go down in droves." Fears in teenage girls manifest in many ways: depression, eating disorders, drugs, casual and confusing sex. Young women, fixated on looks, thinness, and sexuality, are losing themselves in trying to gain approval from peers, grown-ups, and the overheated pop culture that surrounds them.

And yet, through the many case studies I've read, through the stories of women I admire, and, above all, through my own experience with my daughters, again and again I encounter moments of extraordinary strength, courage, and resilience, when fears are confronted, even overcome, and anything seems possible. It was my longing to somehow make these moments last that prompted me to write this book — for my contemporaries, for our mothers, for our daughters.

CLINICAL ANXIETY DISORDERS associated with fear affect more than 20 million Americans. Science has shown that fear is hardwired deep in our lizard brain. What differentiates us from one another are the situations that activate our individual alarms of danger. An armed burglar invading our home? A boyfriend not calling? An odd comment from a friend over lunch? An upcoming wedding toast you're expected to give? Starting a new job? Having to ask your boss for a raise? Saying good-bye to a bad relationship?

Fears — such as fear of snakes, heights, and closed spaces — are not biologically specific to gender, but some do tend to be more prevalent among women than men, including anuptaphobia: fear of staying single; arrhenphobia: fear of men; atelophobia: fear of imperfection; atychiphobia: fear of failure; cacophobia: fear of ugliness; eremophobia: fear of loneliness; gerascophobia: fear of growing old; glossophobia: fear of public speaking; katagelophobia: fear of ridicule; monophobia: fear of being alone; rhytiphobia: fear of getting wrinkles.

Every fear has a name. Whatever it is that frightens you has frightened someone before you. Fear is universal. It touches everyone — but it clearly doesn't stop everyone.

MY OWN BATTLES WITH FEAR

There have been many, many moments of fear in my life, but seven of them were critical — times when the fear was overwhelming but which taught me that it was possible to break through to the other side. To fearlessness.

❖ The first experience of fear I remember was a particularly strange one. I was nine years old. Over dinner one night, my mother started telling my younger sister and me about the time during the Greek civil war, in the 1940s, when she fled to the mountains with two Jewish girls. As part of the Greek Red Cross, she was taking care of wounded soldiers and hiding the girls.

She described the night when German soldiers arrived at their cabin and started to shoot, threatening to kill everyone if the group did not surrender the Jews the Germans suspected (rightly) they were hiding. My mother, who spoke fluent German, stood up and told them categorically to put down their guns, that there were no Jews in their midst. And then she watched the German soldiers lower their guns and walk away. And just hearing it, I remember the fear rising inside me, not just fear for my mother and the danger she faced but fear for myself. How would I ever live up to this standard of fearlessness?

❖   It was 1967, and a group of Greek generals had just staged a coup and established a dictatorship in Athens, where I lived. There was a curfew, and soldiers were stationed at every corner. I was seventeen years old and afraid — torn between the fear that paralyzed me and the desire to ignore the curfew and walk to my economics class so I could fulfill my dream of going to Cambridge University. I ignored the curfew and walked to class.

❖   When I finally got into Cambridge, I instantly fell in love with the Cambridge Union, the university's famed debating society. But, to put it mildly, the Cambridge Union did not instantly fall in love with me. Even before starting my unrequited love affair, I had to overcome the barrier of having a heavy Greek accent in a world where accents really mattered. More important, I had to overcome the fear of criticism and ridicule. If I didn't, I knew I would never be able to speak fearlessly in public.

❖   In 1988, when I published my book on Picasso, I found myself in a battle with the art establishment. My sin was that I had dared criticize Picasso as a man, even while acknowledging his artistic genius. The book was called *Picasso: Creator and Destroyer,* and the art world would not forgive me for exploring the destroyer part — a not inconsiderable facet of Picasso's life. And this, after all, was a biography. My Picasso experience elicited two fears: the fear of being disapproved of by people I liked and respected, and the fear of being caught up in a public controversy.

❖   The most heart-wrenching fear — confronting the possibility of great loss and one's own powerlessness to do anything to stop it — hit me when my younger daughter, Isabella, was not yet one year old. One night, completely unexpectedly, she had a fever-related seizure. I was alone with her. Seeing my baby turn black and blue and realizing she was unable to breathe brought me face-to-face with a chilling fear.

❖   In 2003, I ran for governor in California. During the campaign I was confronted with the fear of being caricatured and misunderstood. Of course, it's in the nature of political campaigns to turn your opponent into a political caricature. But I saw firsthand how different — and how much harder — it is if you're a woman, how much more exposed and vulnerable you feel. I remember sitting at the airport, waiting for a plane to Sacramento, deep in thought about all of this, when a young woman put a note in my hand and then disappeared:

Ms. Huffington,
I didn't want to intrude, but I wanted to thank you for
your statements during the September 24th debate. You
helped make it clear why women in particular should
not vote for Schwarzenegger. While some have com-
plained that your behavior was inappropriate, I realize
that well-behaved women rarely make history. Thanks
for taking on the fight.

Janice Rocco

❖   My mother, who lived with me most of my life — through my marriage, childbirth, and divorce — died in 2000. Her death forced me to confront my deepest fear: living my life without the person who had been its foundation. I did lose her, and I have had to go on without her. But the way she lived her life and faced her death have taught me so much about overcoming fear.

HOW FEAR LIMITS US

Beyond the major moments of fear in our lives, there are many other times we sacrifice our personal truth to go along, be approved of, or just plain be "nice." Because despite all our advances, there's still a huge premium on women being "accommodating" and "team players" who don't "rock the boat." As Marlo Thomas once said, "A man has to be Joe McCarthy to be called ruthless. All a woman has to do is put you on hold." Or, as a friend of mine operating in the treacherous political world of Washington's Beltway told me, "It's good to be a team player, but you also have to know the difference between all of us standing together and all of us jumping off the same cliff." If you let them, the hungry little gremlins of compromise will devour your soul bit by bit and come to dominate your life. They feed the fear of being left out, the fear that survival will be impossible outside the tribe. No wonder fear shoots through our veins, constricting our blood flow and shutting down our creative energy — we are in survival mode.

When we are in the grip of survival thinking, the dominant illusion is that once we vanquish the enemy facing us, overcome the obstacle in front of us, get over the next hill, life will be secure, free of problems, perfect. Then we will be fearless. Then we can start the life we've been planning on. But that long-awaited day never comes because there is always another enemy, another obstacle, another hill.

To live in fear is the worst form of insult to our true selves. By having such a low regard for who we are — for our instincts and abilities and worth — we build a cage around ourselves. To prevent others from shutting us down, we do it for them. Trapped by our own fears, we then pretend that we're incapable of having what we want, forever waiting for others to give us permission to start living. Pretty soon, we start to believe this is the only way.

The most common response to this crisis of self is conformity: "The individual," Erich Fromm writes in *Escape from Freedom,* "ceases to be himself; he adopts entirely the kind of personality offered to him by cultural patterns; and he therefore becomes exactly as all others are and as they expect him to be. . . . This mechanism can be compared with the protective coloring some animals assume."

So, ironically, the woman who appears well adapted may be the one who has simply become most comfortable being governed by her fears, while the "neurotic" one is still gamely struggling to reach fearlessness.

MASTERING FEAR

Fearlessness is not the absence of fear. Rather, it's the mastery of fear. Courage, my compatriot Socrates argues, is the knowledge of what is not to be feared. Which is to say, there are things we *should* be afraid of — we want to stay alive, after all. We will never completely eliminate fear from our lives, but we can definitely get to the point where our fears do not stop us from daring to think new thoughts, try new things, take risks, fail, start again, and be happy.

Fearlessness is about getting up one more time than we fall down. The more comfortable we are with the possibility of falling down, the less worried we are of what people will think if and when we do, the less judgmental of ourselves we are every time we make a mistake, the more fearless we will be, and the easier our journey will become.

I remember once talking to my eight-year-old daughter before a school performance. She kept saying she had butterflies in her stomach because she was afraid to go on the stage. What if, I asked her, the butterflies were actually there because she was excited to go on the stage? She considered the idea. In fact, it became a little joke between us. "I'm not afraid, Mommy," she would say. "I'm excited." The more she repeated it, the more she believed it and the less afraid she was. Since fear is such a primal reaction, making the choice to move forward despite fear is an evolved decision that transcends our animal nature.

IN THE CHAPTERS ahead, I will provide a road map for achieving fearlessness in every aspect of our lives, a straight-to-the-point manifesto on how to be fearless. How to be bold. How to say what we need to say and do what we need to do in a way that has us embracing, not fearing, the reactions of others. Why speaking out is almost always better than silence. How to assess what's holding us back from being our best, most honest selves and what we must do to change. Why the world will be a better place if we actively work for the things we want and believe in.

I have my own key to overcoming fear. I look for the still center in my life and in my self, the place that is not susceptible to life's constant ups and downs. It doesn't mean that I don't lose my head and that I wouldn't rather have success and praise than failure and criticism, but it does mean that I can find my way back to that center, that secure structure of inner support, so that all my negative emotions, and especially my fears, become opportunities to achieve fearlessness. If we can find that greater inner freedom and strength, then we can evolve from a fearful state of living to a state of freedom, trust, and happiness.

We have so much potential, yet we hold ourselves back. If my daughters, and women of all ages, are to take their rightful place in society, they must become fearless. This book is dedicated to them and to that goal.

$\mathcal{N}$ora Ephron on fearlessness

━━━◆◆◆━━━

I THINK OF myself as a fairly brave person. When I was young, I was exceptionally brave about things other girls were wussy about, like snakes and scary movies, and I was very proud of myself.

There's no question in my mind that women tend to be more fearful than men — or else they're allowed by the culture to be more fearful — but I was never really like that: I was a tomboy and an athlete, and my parents were determined that all their children (four girls) be exceptionally brave about their opinions, et cetera. I'm a great admirer of that virtue called manliness, which is highly underrated in women, and to me it includes choosing to be brave rather than fearful.

I probably have a certain amount of impatience with fearfulness and an absolute determination not to be fearful when it's possible to overcome it. But I don't expect to be particularly brave when forced to confront my own death. I wish I were going to be, but I doubt I will.

I used to be afraid of flying, but one day my husband

pointed out to me that it was narcissistic to think that my particular plane was going to crash. That amused me and made sense, so it was sort of the end of my fear of flying.

After September 11, I was full of fear about all the things people were fearful about: subway attacks, germ warfare, smallpox, et cetera. It was a terrifying time; my heart was in my throat. Like everyone I know, I got my doctor to give me a prescription for Cipro in case of an anthrax attack. The Cipro pills are useless now, it's years afterward, but I keep them in my medicine cabinet as a reminder of how frightened I was. But I wasn't a total wuss: I never bought a gas mask. I have friends who did, and I felt about them the way I felt about the girls I grew up with who were afraid of snakes and scary movies.

On the other hand, I should probably admit that now that I'm older, I tend to avoid all scary movies. If I accidentally find myself at a movie that turns scary, I cover my eyes and I don't uncover them until the scary-movie music is over.

I have not seen a snake lately, so I have no idea how I would respond. Although I recently killed a mouse with a broom, so I would probably be all right.

Nora Ephron's latest book is I Feel Bad About My Neck: And Other Thoughts on Being a Woman.

Fearless About the Body

---❦---

The Perfection of Imperfection

THE MOST INTIMATE relationship we'll ever have is with our own body. It's the headquarters of our fears and anxieties. It's also the cause of many of them. Which is why we can never really be fearless until we stop judging our looks and accept them.

I've always loved Orinthia's classic, brimming-with-chutzpah speech in George Bernard Shaw's *The Apple Cart.* Having seen the play a number of times, I've noticed that it's actually better when Orinthia is played by an actress who is not conventionally beautiful, because then it makes the point more clearly that Orinthia's confidence in herself comes from a deeper place than her looks or her achievements. The king, with whom she's having an affair, challenges her: "It must be magnificent to have the conscience of a goddess without ever doing a thing to justify it."

She replies: "Give me a goddess's work to do; and I will do it. I will even stoop to a queen's work if you will share the throne with me. But do not pretend that people become great by doing great things. They do great things because they are great, if the great things come along. But they are great just the same when the great things do not come along. If I never did anything but sit in this room and powder my face and tell you what a clever fool you are, I should still be heavens high above the millions of common women who do their domestic duty, and sacrifice themselves, and run trade departments and all the rest of the vulgarities. . . . Thank God my self-consciousness is something nobler than vulgar conceit in having done something. It is what I am, not what I do, that you must worship in me."

Granted, it would be nicer if all this confidence were directed at something a little nobler than getting the king to marry her. But the essence of Orinthia's declaration is that fearlessness and confidence in ourselves come not from what we do, or what we accomplish, or what we wear, or how we look, but from a deep and complete acceptance of ourselves. We are who we are no matter what we look like or what we achieve.

KEEPING UP APPEARANCES

For eons, beauty has been a big measure, often the only measure, of a woman's worth. The urge to attract seems to be hardwired in us — even a biological necessity. In her book *Survival of the Prettiest: The Science of Beauty,* Harvard psychologist Nancy Etcoff writes that "beauty is a universal part of human experience. . . . It provokes pleasure, rivets attention, and impels actions that help ensure the survival of our genes." Across different cultures and different eras, as long as human beings have existed, beauty has been at the heart of how women have been treated. It has also been central to women's survival, since beautiful women often attract strong protectors. It's no wonder it became a paramount preoccupation for us.

Did you know that over seven thousand years ago red pigments were already being used as lip color? The beauty products industry may, in fact, be the world's second-oldest profession — if you believe the old axiom about the world's oldest. Today, according to Etcoff, between the L'Oréals and the Clairols and all the rest, some five hundred different shades of blond hair dye are manufactured to please the estimated 40 percent of women in the United States alone who add blond to their hair. Some two thousand jars of skin care products and nearly fifteen hundred tubes of lipstick are sold every minute. "More money," Etcoff writes, "is spent on beauty than on education or social services."

FEARS ABOUT PEERS

Insecurity about our looks comes into full bloom in adolescence and is now almost a rite of passage. I still cringe at how self-conscious I was as a teenager. Let's start with the fact that I was freakishly tall for a Greek girl, standing five ten at thirteen, when my classmates were five nothing. I remember the trauma of being excluded from the school parade, which included all the tallest girls at the school, because I was, yes, too tall. Add to that unruly curly hair, heavy acne, and thick glasses, and, well, you get the not-so-pretty picture. I was only happy when I was lost in my books.

The rest of the time I was consumed by fears that I would never have a boyfriend, never be attractive to boys. I kept comparing myself to all my beautiful, diminutive classmates as I towered over them in my exquisite awkwardness. I kept getting A's in school, but it didn't matter to me because all I really cared about was how I looked.

The good grades were my ticket out, but I still took a lot of these fears with me to Cambridge. I began dating, but was also constantly doubting myself. Most of my happiness at Cambridge came not from my relationships but from beginning to master public speaking, debating, and the clash of ideas. It took me many years before I would find myself as a woman.

THE CRITIC IN THE MIRROR

Imagine if someone invented a little tape recorder that we could attach to our brains to record everything we tell ourselves — a TiVo for our inner dialogue. What we'd discover is that not even our worst enemies talk about us the way we talk about ourselves. The negative self-talk starts as soon as we wake up — sometimes even before. It revs up when we take that first look in the mirror or get on a scale or put on a pair of pants that fits too snugly. "Oh, my God, I look awful . . . another wrinkle here — I hope that's just from the pillow. . . . Did I put these pants in the dryer? Can't . . . seem to . . . zip them." On and on it goes, as we fret over every blemish, every extra pound. It's like having the world's worst roommate — one who's around 24/7.

Last spring I took my teenage daughters to see Eve Ensler's play *The Good Body*. It was fascinating to be with them while we watched one woman's journey from fear about every flaw to fearlessness and acceptance of her body with all its imperfections.

"Why write a play about my stomach?" asks Ensler in the play's preface. "Maybe because my stomach is one thing I feel I have control over, or maybe because I have hoped that my stomach is something I could get control over. Maybe because I see how my stomach has come to occupy my attention, I see how other women's stomachs or butts or thighs or hair or skin have come to occupy their attention, so that we have very little left for the war in Iraq — or much else, for that matter."

But self-consciousness about our abs or butts or faces isn't just an individual preoccupation, it's almost a social dictate. As Naomi Wolf observes in *The Beauty Myth,* one side effect of the feminist revolution was that society's emphasis shifted from expecting us to maintain the perfect home as a housewife to expecting us to maintain the perfect face, hair, and body as a working woman.

And if we are momentarily diverted from thoughts about our looks, there are dozens of women's magazines to get us back on track. "Why can't you," they implicitly (and sometimes explicitly) ask, "be like the superwomen we feature — tall, thin, juggling a career and children without ever breaking a sweat, looking fearless, impeccable, properly exfoliated, moisturized, and put together?"

But where is that superwoman? I can certainly tell you she's never been seen around my house. And even if she were to show up, my inner-dialogue roommate would be sure to find some "areas of improvement" she could concern herself with.

If there's one thing all of this shows, it's how successful women have been at internalizing the notion that they've been put on this earth to please men. And every time we threaten to finally shuck this idea off, we find a way to somehow reembrace it. As Maureen Dowd writes, "It took only a few decades to create a brazen new world where the highest ideal is to acknowledge your inner slut."

THE TREADMILL OF COMPARISONS

Our fears about our looks naturally lead us to compare ourselves endlessly with others — and others are all, of course, endlessly comparing themselves to us. It's a fear-and-self-doubt perpetual-motion machine: Why can't we just be as pretty, as sexy, as athletic, as young as her or her or her, or the hundreds of women looking at us from magazines, billboards, and TV screens?

Our culture is obsessed with glamour, attractiveness, fashion, hipness, and youth. So our internal pressures to look perfect are constantly reinforced by airbrushed images of movie stars and models ministered to by a retinue of stylists, makeup artists, and plastic surgeons.

If it is your goal to compete with these immaculate images, you will never win. And even if it's not your goal, that doesn't mean you're immune to the cultural noise around you. The average woman sees four hundred to six hundred advertisements per day, and by the age of seventeen, the average person will have been exposed to about 250,000 commercial messages. Worse, according to the 2002 book *Advertising to the American Woman: 1900–1999,* one of every eleven commercials communicates a direct message about beauty. Add in the endless *indirect* messages being sent and you can see what we're up against!

The outside world barrages us with these incessant messages and images; it's not going to stop, and we can't control it. But what we can do is exert some control on the inside. We can find the strength, and the fearlessness, to refuse to be pulled onto this treadmill of comparisons.

THE PRICE ISN'T RIGHT

With so much internal and external pressure to be beautiful, it's no wonder women go to such absurd lengths to achieve the goal of perfection. Fear that we will not measure up leads to stifling conformity as we try to squeeze ourselves into the mold.

Conformity is not the only cost of our obsession with our bodies, however. There are psychological and financial price tags as well, not to mention the toll on our physical health.

More than half of American women have gone on a diet at some point in their lives. That's probably because the three-quarters of women who are of normal weight consider themselves heavy. And then there's the financial cost: We spend some $33 billion a year (yes, *billion*) on diet books, diet foods, diet programs, and diet accessories.

Worse, disturbing numbers of women — vastly more than ever — are basically starving themselves. National Institute of Mental Health statistics show that over 3 percent of women suffer from bulimia and over 4 percent from anorexia. This trend takes the fear of fat to a fatal extreme.

If we can't starve our way to beauty, many of us turn to costly medical interventions. In 2005 alone, according to the American Society of Plastic Surgeons, more than 10 million cosmetic surgery procedures — including liposuction, "nose jobs," breast implants, eyelid surgery, and "tummy tucks" — were performed in this country. That's more than a 10 percent increase from the previous year. And those numbers don't even include the close to 9 million relatively minor procedures, such as face-freezing Botox injections.

An especially ugly truth is that women are going under the knife at a younger and younger age. Thousands of teenagers are getting breast implants, even taking out loans if they can't afford them. According to a Texas A&M study reported by Richard Conniff in *The Natural History of the Rich:* "It is customary for upper-class parents in the Dallas–Fort Worth area to give their daughters breast implant surgery as a high school graduation gift. It is explicitly recognized by both parents and daughters that the young women will get more dates and be more popular in college if they have larger breasts. As one student put it: 'Among the wealthier families, the boys get hot cars for graduation, and the girls get big breasts.'"

And if changing our bodies isn't enough, we're resorting in larger and larger numbers to changing our brains, with mood-altering drugs. A 2004 Centers for Disease Control study found that one in ten women take antidepressants such as Prozac. The National Sleep Foundation (yes, there is one) found that 63 percent of women experience symptoms of insomnia several nights a week. And one health care company reported that in 2004, 58 percent more women than men took prescription drugs to sleep. Sure, there are plenty of legitimate reasons to take these medications, but can anyone doubt that part of the reason for their popularity is that women need a way to shut down and get some respite from our constant fears and anxieties?

ON BECOMING FEARLESS ABOUT HOW WE LOOK

The first step to becoming fearless about our physical appearance is knowing that our fears of inadequacy are manufactured and mass-marketed. The fear-generating messages of perfection we measure ourselves against come not from Moses on the mountaintop but from the multibillion-dollar cosmetics and fashion industries whose profits are directly tied to our levels of insecurity.

As Jean Kilbourne writes in *Can't Buy My Love: How Advertising Changes the Way We Think and Feel*, the reason so much is spent on market research and advertising is because it works. Marketers know that if they team up with the multibillion-dollar entertainment industry, they can not only sell us fantasies but also then sell us the products we think will help us realize them.

That's only half the story, however. We are, after all, the ones perpetuating the game of comparisons. The urge to compare, to see how we're doing relative to others, is a part of the human condition. But we can enlarge our perspective to dilute the power of our narrow, self-destructive comparisons. I know this is hard, but if we can't completely stop playing the comparison game, we can at least start changing whom we compare ourselves to. Instead of comparing ourselves to Angelina Jolie, how about comparing ourselves to a victim of Hurricane Katrina, a woman who lost her legs fighting in Iraq, or a woman diagnosed with breast cancer? They're out there, too. When we do this, we are sure to tap into our reserves of empathy and gratitude instead of our endless self-judgments, fears, and jealousies.

It was only when I began observing the critical voices inside me rather than giving in to them that I could start to take control over them. Instead of being drained by the negative self-talk, I found myself amused by it the way you are by a naughty child. We have a choice about what to do with the messages we hear. We may not be able to tune them out entirely, but we don't have to let them run the show.

For example, if the voice is saying something specific, such as "I want to slim down," "I need more exercise," or "It might be fun to get highlights," then fine, go ahead and do it. But if the voice is just mindlessly nit-picking and running us down, we have a responsibility to lower the volume. If we let these voices deplete our energies, they will. Since the comparison game is a game that no one can win, why play in the first place?

Putting our energies into a creative project can help put an end to our obsessions with ourselves. Actress Rosanna Arquette confessed to "stressing" about having a "chicken neck" as she approached forty. But the obsession to look perfect — all the more intense in her profession — no longer consumed her after she reached out to others and produced a film called *Searching for Debra Winger,* about balancing motherhood and art. "It set me on my path to stay positive," she told me, "to connect with other women, my tribe. We have to cut out competition, because we are all on the same path of fearlessness, to be truly who we are, and this is our birthright! It's time we support and love each other in what we want to do in life so we can look at each other and know we are safe. Let's celebrate each other's individuality, blessings — and cellulite."

SELF-CONFIDENCE IS THE ULTIMATE TURN-ON
I have many women friends in their fifties who look better now than they looked in their forties. Yes, they take care of them-

selves. But truly, the main change is an inner one. If power, according to Henry Kissinger, is the ultimate aphrodisiac for women, confidence is a great aphrodisiac for men. The French even have a phrase for it: *jolie laide*. Women described as *jolie laide* are not classically beautiful, but they radiate a kind of magnetism that goes beyond their specific features.

As fashion reporter Karen Burshtein writes: "The term translates literally as 'pretty ugly' but could more charitably be rendered as 'oddly beautiful.' The *jolie laide* represents an idea of beauty wherein a hint of imperfection enhances a woman's appearance and makes her more interesting to look at. . . . In the end, she is more alluring, more captivating, than a conventional beauty."

Think about Sarah Jessica Parker as Carrie Bradshaw on *Sex and the City*. Who cares about Parker's lack of a button nose when you have her character's quick wit, quirky fashion choices, and overall adorability? Or look at plus-size, multitalented Queen Latifah, whose ample curves, mischievous smile, winsome confidence, and personal warmth are all part of her commanding presence.

In a 2005 *Allure* magazine survey on attitudes about beauty, men and women both ranked Oprah Winfrey, Sophia Loren, and Meryl Streep among the most beautiful celebrities. In addition, two-thirds of the men surveyed said that they would rather their significant others did not have plastic surgery.

While it was still a work in progress, I posted parts of this book on my blog on the Huffington Post and asked readers for their comments and personal stories. I got many great responses. One of them came from Larry Sankey: "I think the women who are called *jolie laide* are simply those not overly concerned with how they look. Even physically beautiful women who are too concerned with their looks come off as insecure and therefore somehow unattractive."

Hollywood hasn't gotten the memo. I experienced an illustration of this at an Oscar week party in 2006. There was plenty to gawk at, but I could not take my eyes off the spectacle of Hugh Hefner and the three pneumatically endowed platinum blondes on his arm. I know it's all part of his shtick, but seriously, the guy is actually shuffling now. You wonder if with all that Viagra coursing through his system he's got enough blood circulating above his waist.

But even more horrifying were the women. At some point they must have been lovely. And most likely, they still would be — but we'll never know. That level of heavy construction and demolition can never be undone. Sadly, there's no such thing yet as reverse plastic surgery — there's only . . . more plastic surgery.

I know there's a lot of talk about how America can't manufacture anything anymore, but there seems to be an endless supply of these manufactured women. I guess Bangladesh and India haven't found a way to undercut us on this yet. And good for them.

The only thing that could take me away from the Hefner spectacle was the appearance at the party of a true Hollywood freak: a beautiful, non-twenty-something woman who had not had any plastic surgery at all! I don't know how she got past the security guards, but there she was. It was Connie Nielsen, the Danish actress who starred in *Ice Harvest, One Hour Photo,* and *Gladiator.* She was sitting at an adjoining table to the Hefner-Bots. As I was talking to her, it was impossible not to note the contrast. She's forty, and still in possession of her own face. She is passionate, confident, and proudly herself. I'm hoping it's the beginning of a renaissance of soulful women with no face-lifts.

THE TRUE BEAUTY SECRET

Ultimately, the greatest beauty secret is to live out our passions and connect with our own spirit.

The 2004 Dove Campaign for Real Beauty Report, an extensive survey of women of various ages and nationalities, found that "women feel beautiful when they are fully engaged in meaningful life activities. More than half of women say they feel beautiful when they help others (54%); spend time with their children (53%); achieve success (46%); are physically active (46%); do something artistic (39%); enjoy a hobby (39%); or dance (35%). Surprisingly, activities that are directly related to beauty, such as shopping for beauty care products (21%) and looking at fashion magazines (17%), were less likely to make women feel beautiful."

The report goes on: "Spirituality also plays a key role in helping women feel beautiful. Seventy-five percent of women agree that beauty comes from a woman's spirit and love of life, not from her looks. Additionally . . . 42% said that one of the times they feel most beautiful is when they attend a religious service." And the survey was not about when women felt *good* but about when they actually felt *beautiful.*

BE GOOD TO YOUR BODY

Finding your inner beauty doesn't mean ignoring your physical self. I remember that when I first started on my spiritual journey in the 1970s, I put on twenty pounds. My excuse was "Who cares what I look like? It's all about connecting to God and spirit, right?" Right. But I've learned it's not an either/or, body/spirit division. As I began to integrate the different parts of myself, it became clear that taking care of the temple in which the soul resides is a legitimate priority. And, yes, it's undeniable how different you feel when you do all the obvious things, like eat right, exercise, and get enough sleep.

STOP THE WAR WITH FOOD

Growing up in Greece, we ate lots of fresh fruit and vegetables, a great deal of fish, and a seemingly endless amount of olive oil. A healthy diet by anyone's measure. But healthier still was the attitude toward food itself — very different from the attitude here, where women have come to view food as the enemy. We starve ourselves, deny ourselves carbohydrates, rid our systems of all fat, and then, when we feel we "deserve" it or have earned it after weeks of denial, we turn 180 degrees and indulge in binge-eating. Every woman I know has tried — and then rebelled against — a harsh, strict diet. I speak from experience, having tried them all. The Beverly Hills diet, the all-brown-rice diet, the grapefruit diet, the cabbage soup diet, the no carbs, no fat, indeed no calories diet. No, I'm not exaggerating. When I was living in London in the late seventies, I even tried the water diet — partly because I was tired of living on cheddar cheese and crackers, partly to shed some pounds, and partly because starving my body seemed like a good shortcut to touching the spirit. Fortunately I realized sooner rather than later that treating physical reality as a dispensable illusion was no less misleading than dismissing spiritual reality as a hallucination. Anyway, by the time I ended my fast, I could, blindfolded, tell the difference between the various brands of bottled water I was drinking.

Mireille Guiliano has it right in *French Women Don't Get Fat: The Secret of Eating for Pleasure:* "French women simply do not suffer the terror of kilos that afflicts so many of their American sisters. All the chatter about diets I hear at cocktail parties in America would make any French woman cringe. In France, we don't talk about 'diets,' certainly not with strangers. . . . Mainly we spend our social time talking about what we enjoy: feelings, family, hobbies, philosophy, politics, culture, and, yes, food, especially food (but never diets)."

One final word of advice: Never get up from the table feeling stuffed or guilty, but also never get up without feeling satisfied. Lisa Sanders concludes in *The Perfect Fit Diet* that any diet that doesn't allow you to have this feeling of satiation will fail. Different diets trigger the satiation hormones in the brain differently in different people, which is why no one diet works for everybody.

WORK IT OUT

When I hit forty — which is also when I had my second child — I had to make some big decisions about my body. My wishes went in one direction, but my Greek genes were taking me in a completely different one. And the latter path was laid out pretty clearly in the form of my wonderful Greek mother, who at the time was making an utterly graceful transition from dresses to muumuus. She had no interest in doing battle with time and nature.

Her daughter, however, did. My main challenge was to find a

form of exercise that I would stick with. That's how I discovered hiking with friends. Not only did I enjoy it, but it soon became a passion. Three or four times a week, instead of going to lunch, my friends and I go on a hike. We observe a strict policy: Everything that is said on the hike stays on the hike — or "in the vault," as we call it. The other rule is that the one — or ones — in better shape talk on the way up and the others on the way down. Recently, we did a birthday hike for a friend. We hiked to Inspiration Point at Will Rogers Park in Los Angeles, toting along backpacks filled with healthy food. We put a tablecloth on a picnic table, opened individual minibottles of champagne, toasted the birthday girl, and feasted on cheese, vegetables, and fruit — okay, and on some dark chocolate.

You might enjoy running, swimming, biking, or playing tennis, but if you're not a naturally athletic person, and I'm not, you've got to make exercise fun; otherwise it will never become part of your life. Along with my morning hikes, yoga has become another form of exercise I've grown to love. Even better, it's a love I can share with my younger daughter, Isabella. Through yoga, I've become stronger, more flexible, more aware of my body, and — a big bonus — closer to my daughter.

Above all, yoga has taught me the power of breathing: observing it, slowing it, controlling it (along with my stress reactions). Yes, it can be hard to let go of distractions, as yoga requires. Our teacher, Scott Hobbs, still laughs when I try to sneak a peek at my BlackBerry in the downward-facing-dog position. But he never tires of repeating that "we can survive weeks without food, days without water, but mere minutes without breathing."

We need to breathe not only to live but to feel good. Breathing consciously helps us find the strength and energy to live fearlessly. "The first step in improving your breathing," Scott tells us, "is to become aware of it. Constantly." The way we breathe sends messages to our body. Are we relaxed? Afraid? Uptight? Nervous? Insecure?

Joan Witkowski teaches breathing coordination, and through her I've learned a simple technique of counting on a long exhale until your breathing becomes deeper and you stop holding or forcing the breath. The marvelous thing about it is that it takes only a few minutes in the middle of your day to recharge and restore.

Yoga and conscious breathing get us more in touch with what our bodies have to tell us about both our physical and mental states. Playwright and actress Anna Deavere Smith believes fervently in the inevitable connection of mind and body as a source of creativity. She told me that swimming and training with boxers have taught her how the body and the imagination click together.

"We are all 'bodies' of knowledge," she says. "The more in tune we are spiritually, the more connected we are, and the more this is revealed in our bodies. This all started for me with my yoga teacher years ago, who taught me that it's the process, the learning of the movement that counts. When I told her I was afraid of doing a shoulder stand she replied, 'It really has more to do with learning a movement,' giving me right there an ingredient for fearlessness."

It's so simple that it's easy to miss: When we feel strong, when our bodies are healthy, we don't feel as vulnerable as when we are weak and out of shape. It's harder to feel fearless when we become breathless climbing up a flight of stairs. It's amazing how I can take on something challenging after a good yoga class or an energetic hike. My mind is awake, my body is limber, and I'm ready for anything.

TO SLEEP, PERCHANCE TO DREAM

I've saved possibly the most important step for last: Get enough sleep. In my personal experience, there is no question that it's much harder to be fearless when you're sleep deprived. I become more moody, more reactive, more anxious, and more shaky both physically and emotionally. As a result, I try to get seven to eight hours of sleep a night as often as possible. And the difference is astounding. I'm much more productive and much happier than when I squeeze four or five more hours of sleep-deprived wakefulness out of my day.

Sleep deprivation is one area in which the United States unfortunately leads the way. Some statistics:

❖   A 2005 poll by the National Sleep Foundation reports that 75 percent of Americans experience sleep problems.

❖   The National Highway Traffic Safety Administration says that drowsiness causes 100,000 crashes a year in the United States, killing 1,500 people.

❖   Sleep problems have a ripple effect. When disturbed by a partner's sleep problems, you lose almost an hour of sleep a night — more than three hundred hours a year!

❖   Nearly 25 percent of adults say they have sex less often or have lost interest because they are too sleepy.

Beyond these quantifiable consequences is the pernicious impact sleep deprivation has on the quality of our lives, from our temper to our judgment.

I'm not suggesting cutting short a fun evening or leaving the wedding reception early because you need to get your eight hours. Just remember to keep your eyes open to the benefits of getting enough shut-eye. One of the benefits for me is how much less food I need. Nothing sends us to food faster than fatigue — especially when we have to keep going. And after scarfing down those cookies and feeling bloated, we just feel tired again in about twenty minutes.

LOVE YOU JUST THE WAY YOU ARE

Ultimately, true fearlessness comes from loving the body you were born with, which is inseparable from your individuality.

Miranda Spencer, a writer and editor in her late forties, told me, "I'm fully aware of my bodily imperfections, but I have an odd affection for them. My thighs are huge, but dammit, they're *my* huge thighs. My nose is a little long, but I can see my family history in this face, and it makes me feel closer to my parents and grandparents. It's *my* long nose. I wish I could tweak my appearance by toning up or losing ten pounds, but I wouldn't overhaul it. I like recognizing myself in the mirror. I'd like to see an *improved* me, but not anyone *other than* me."

We all come to our own version of acceptance about our bodies and our appearance. But the sooner we realize that our happiness and the meaning of our life are not by-products of how we look, the sooner we can move to fearlessness.

$\mathscr{S}$ue Smalley on fearlessness

AT FORTY-SEVEN I was fighting aging, death, and dying with a vengeance, compulsively exercising to look good, getting Botox (twice), contemplating plastic surgery. I was feeling old, looking "old," and doing what I could to hang on to a thin and firm body and a face without lines. Then I had a complete shift.

It began with my facing the profound fear of dying. A tiny freckle turned out to be an in situ melanoma (the earliest stage of this deadly skin cancer). In an attempt to avoid death, I began a journey of self-discovery and healing. I began to recognize my habitual patterns, used all my energy to change my habits, and introduced a healthy diet, massage, acupuncture, yoga, and meditation into my life.

These were all new experiences, and they led to a new awareness of our interconnectedness and our changing nature, and to the recognition that death is inevitable and trying to hang on to life or hang on to things only brings about pain and suffering.

As a geneticist, I could see evidence of all this directly in our DNA. The peculiar thing about this awareness is that from it arises a deep sense of connection to living and nonliving things, to something bigger than oneself, and to an emerging sense of compassion. For how can one hurt or harm that of which one is a part? At forty-seven I became aware of this truth, and in that awareness I found genuine happiness. I became more joyful, more calm, more connected, kinder, and more generous.

I now welcome aging, death, and dying as part of the great cycle of life. And through this welcoming came a new kind of beauty. I felt the beauty of life as it is, each moment as it arises, and the infinite glow of being part of it, rather than needing to be special, different, unique, famous. I now feel the joy and beauty in being part of a giant web of interconnectedness.

I have a photo of me at forty-seven and one of me today, four years later. And if I put them side by side, you would swear I must have had work done, because I look so much better now. I may have the same number of facial lines, the same body weight, the same facial structure, but physically I look different.

I do still dye my hair and blow-dry it, and I work out, and I'm careful of what I eat, but these are part of my appreciation for who I am. It's all about loving oneself — but one's true self, not a facade of who we are.

When you get in touch with your true self, that's when your inner beauty can reveal itself.

Sue Smalley is a professor of psychiatry at UCLA, specializing in genetics and ADHD.

$\mathcal{F}$earless in Love

Knowing and Being Known

IT'S NO SECRET that women's fears about love are different from men's. We tend to crave a relationship the way we hunger for food and water. We think we can't live without one — we don't feel safe, we don't feel complete, we don't feel as if we're doing what we were put on this earth to do. This is our survival instinct kicking in.

But it isn't real — or at least it isn't really what it appears to be. Survival behavior can be triggered by the fear of losing anything that we perceive as being part of our identity: the approval of our parents, our looks, a cherished keepsake, and of course a relationship. Once the fight-or-flight instinct has been triggered, it exercises a manual override, and everything not connected to the perceived danger is shoved aside.

FEAR OF BEING ALONE
The fear of being alone underlies all other love-related fears. It's the überfear.

When we feel chronically incomplete, we figure the best way to solve this, at least temporarily, is through a relationship. And so we'll do anything to make one work or to pretend it's working. This leads to an awful lot of twisted behaviors. I'm sure we all have our own personal cringe-worthy outtakes reel.

One woman I know got divorced after she could no longer deal with her husband's multiple affairs. Shortly after her separation, she began dating a colleague who had listened patiently to her stories about her philandering husband. Even though her friends all urged her to take some breathing space, she threw herself into this new relationship. She couldn't be alone, she said. Soon, however, her colleague, now boyfriend, started making excuses for why he couldn't show up at certain events. It turned out that he was living with another woman the whole time. Most would have thought leaving him would be the only rational thing to do, but she, in fear, continued to date him! When asked why, she simply answered, "Well, it's better than being alone."

In her book *Women Who Love Too Much*, Robin Norwood writes that some women think "being in love means being in pain." Feeling inadequate, and often longing for the love they didn't get as children, they are drawn to dysfunctional relationships that mirror the frustrations of their past and become compelled to make them work, against all odds or common sense — and however intense the pain.

This dynamic can easily lead to physically abusive relationships. We look at such relationships — especially those where the abuse happens repeatedly — and wonder why the woman doesn't just leave. But if you understand women's deep fear of being alone, it's not a huge mystery.

Sometimes this fear is a practical one, as philanthropist and children's rights activist Cheryl Saban told me: "I was in an abusive marriage and wanted out. But I was afraid I wouldn't be able to support my two young daughters. I wanted to leave, but I stayed in the relationship years more than I should have. I felt alone, I felt like I'd sold myself out — I felt like a loser."

While I was writing my biography of Picasso, I encountered many beautiful, talented women who stayed with the great artist years longer than they should have. In fact, Picasso used to boast that he liked to take goddesses and turn them into doormats. It was a boast he lived up to. Two of the important women in his life committed suicide; two others got away with only nervous breakdowns. The only one who escaped, Françoise Gilot, was able to go on and build a new life and love other men, including Jonas Salk, whom she married. I met her when I moved to New York, and I learned a lot from her about fearlessness in relationships.

On Françoise's thirtieth birthday, in November 1951, Picasso's present to her was to inform her that "any girl of eighteen is more beautiful than you." (Happy birthday!) What Françoise described to me was a process instantly recognizable to anyone who has ever made compromises to stay in a relationship that is no longer healthy or fulfilling.

She gradually learned to shut off a part of herself so that what Picasso said or did no longer hurt as much. "There was a crippling that took place," she told me, "but at first I did not even notice it. I had tried to stop the pain of the betrayal I felt, and in the process I had amputated a part of myself and of our relationship." She had been brought up to place a high premium on dignity and self-control. Those traits can serve you well, but they can also be used as an excuse for self-denial. In Françoise's case, this meant saying nothing about her pain, expressing none of her needs. "You go silent on me," Picasso complained once, "become sarcastic, a little bitter, aloof and cold. I'd like just once to see you spill your guts out on the table, laugh, cry — play *my* game." But she did not. Instead, she shut herself down and grew more and more distant.

And of course, as it always happens, things didn't stay bad. They got worse. When Picasso told her that he wanted to leave the south of France and spend some time alone in Paris, Françoise, putting aside her pride, asked him again and again to take her with him. He refused, and for the first time she warned him that the more time they spent apart, the greater the chance she would leave him. He laughed at the very idea: "Nobody leaves a man like me. Besides, people who threaten things like that never do them."

So he left for Paris. Despite all the defenses, all the walls she had built for herself, despite all the self-abnegation, Françoise was shattered. "Suddenly," she told me, "I found myself on the other side of the Magic Mountain that my deep love for him had created. At the beginning of our relationship, he often talked about ascending our Magic Mountain together. And even after all the disillusionment and the pain of the last year, there was still something left of the Magic Mountain. Now I was on the other side of it, and during the weeks Pablo was in Paris I realized that I was out of love and that the Magic Mountain had disappeared."

But even as Picasso continued to mistreat her, giving her more and more reasons to leave, she was still too full of fear to make the final break and face not just his wrath, but an outraged world that, she surmised, would blame her for the breakup. She was right. For finally doing what so many other women before her couldn't do, Françoise was accused of selfishness, of wickedness, and, worst of all, of having failed to sufficiently understand and genuflect before the genius of our time.

Whether you're with a genius or an ordinary man, it takes courage to walk away. Sometimes you just have to get sick and tired of being sick and tired to be willing to face an uncertain future rather than stay in a painful present. That's what Françoise did, and her story is a powerful inspiration for other women.

THE PLEASER PROBLEM

One of women's biggest fears is the disapproval of the men in their lives. And the price we are willing to pay to avoid this often includes being untrue to ourselves.

I speak from experience. For a long time this was definitely my biggest fear, starting with my first really important relationship. I was twenty-one when I first met Bernard Levin on a panel for *Face the Music,* a British guess-the-music TV show. He was forty-two. I was there as a curiosity — a young woman with a foreign accent, elected president of the Cambridge Union. He was there as the celebrated columnist for the *London Times,* an intellectual with an encyclopedic knowledge of music and pretty much everything else. Except me. He knew nothing about me. But I knew a lot about him. I'd had a major intellectual crush on him ever since I had discovered his writings while at Cambridge. I had devoured his book *The Pendulum Years* and would meticulously clip his columns, underline them, and save them in a file (no, I did not put pressed flowers in the file, but I might as well

have). So when I found out that he was on the panel, I was reduced to an inarticulate bundle of fears. I'm still amazed that in
my fog, I actually managed to recognize Schumann's Fourth
Symphony.

At the end of the taping, he asked me out to dinner for the
following week. All I remember is that I spent the week in a state
of high anxiety, prepping, primping, getting myself up-to-date
on Northern Ireland, recent developments in the Soviet Union,
and the latest Wagner recordings. I had so many fear butterflies
during dinner, I basically just rearranged the food on my plate. I
must have bored him to death, because he made sure our second
date didn't involve a lot of talking. He took me to Covent Garden to see Wagner's *Mastersingers*. As you might guess by now, I
spent the time between the dinner and the opera date reading all
about *The Mastersingers* — and, considering more has been written about Wagner than anyone else except Jesus Christ, that
meant a lot of reading.

That week we started a relationship that would last until the
end of 1980, when I left London to move to New York. In many
ways Bernard was, in fact, the reason I left London. I was thirty
by then and still deeply in love with him, but I longed to have
children. He, on the other hand, never wanted to have children
or get married. What was touching about him was that he saw
this rejection not as a badge of independence and freedom but as
a character flaw, a by-product of his deepest fears. He even wrote
about it. And the fear he describes is by no means confined to
men: "What fear of revealing, of vulnerability, of being human,
grips us so fiercely, and above all why? What is it that, down there
in the darkness of the psyche, cries its silent 'No' to the longing

for 'Yes'?" For him this "No" often coincided with a retreat into depression — which he described as "that dark lair where the sick soul's desire for solitude turns into misanthropy."

No wonder he loved cats so much. "Above all," he wrote once, "I love the detachment of cats, their willingness to be loved but not to respond beyond a certain, very clearly defined point; no cat ever gave its entire heart to any human being."

I have since talked with dozens of women trapped in relationships like mine, in which the man is not able or willing to match our longing for a deeper intimacy. And however necessary it is, it's incredibly hard and painful to extricate ourselves. Instead we keep trying to make things better — by which we mean make *ourselves* better. I know how hard I worked to gain Bernard's approval. Because on some level I feared that I had fallen short — that if it weren't for *my* shortcomings, we would be spending our lives together. Rationally I knew that his intimacy and commitment issues were *his* and had little or nothing to do with me, but irrationally I feared that it was I who wasn't enough. And as a result, I stayed long after it was clear that I was no longer being true to myself.

In fact, I still marvel at what reserves of fearlessness I must have tapped into to be able to leave him. And not just to leave him — the first big love of my life, as well as a mentor as a writer and a role model as a thinker — but also to leave London and to change continents. But I had to. Our lives in London were so inextricably intertwined that I couldn't live there any longer. A quarter of a century later, I can still feel how painful that decision was.

My biography of Maria Callas, published in 1980 — the year

I left — is dedicated to Bernard: "Without his unfailing support and understanding," I wrote in the acknowledgments, "and without the long hours he spent reading, criticizing, and improving, I wondered sometimes whether there would be a book at all."

FEAR OF REJECTION

Maria Callas is a classic example of a woman who gave her life over to a man and didn't leave. She touched thousands through her music but then proceeded to devote the rest of her life to not losing Aristotle Onassis. What started off as a mutual love affair turned into something unhealthy and one-sided. She ended up sacrificing herself and her gifts for fear of being left by this one man.

If there was a signature theme to most of the operas Callas was famous for, it was this: love lost, love betrayed, love abandoned. She tasted fame, success, and wealth — but all she truly cared about was being loved by Onassis. And what in fact happened in her own life's story is that he left her for Jackie Kennedy, and in the end she died of a broken heart.

The worldwide public adulation wasn't enough — it was as if only Onassis could validate her. And in her relentless pursuit of validation, Callas allowed herself to be treated like a doormat. Once that spiral got started, the end was obvious. If it hadn't been Jackie, it would have been someone else. "You are just a larynx," Onassis would say to Maria, and she put up with it. Why? What makes women do that?

How often do we as women move heaven and earth to structure our lives around getting a man to love us, to accept us, to honor us, to just like us — all so we can feel okay about ourselves? Intelligent, smart, talented, hardworking women allow themselves to be lost in the quest for one man's approval. They put up with his affairs, his whims, his indifference, his distance, his disregard, his contempt. "Alas, our frailty is the cause, not we! For such as we are made of, such we be," says Viola in Shakespeare's *Twelfth Night*.

When did we become frail, give up our strength, our spirit, our wisdom, to submit and compromise who we are out of fear of being alone or out of fear of not being with the mythical "one"? What are we afraid of? What might befall us if, God forbid, we stop trying to please a man? Clearly we fear being rejected.

And this fear affects us even when our relationships are healthy and satisfying. We fear that at some point, even if we have managed to please, we will be seen as lacking and inadequate. The man will discover that we are simply not good enough or pretty enough or sexy enough or young enough, and we'll be thrown on the reject heap, traded in for a younger, more desirable model. It might happen, it might not, but whether or not it does has very little to do with all the time — sometimes years — we give over to *worrying* that it might happen. Have you noticed that worrying doesn't stop it from happening? And indeed, that we worry about many things that never happen? As Montaigne put it, "There have been many terrible misfortunes in my life, but most of them never happened."

Sadly, our fear of being inadequate isn't one that diminishes with accumulated experience. On the contrary, as we get older, we worry that with wrinkles or spreading waistlines we will not be able to hold on to our partners.

Fear of rejection manifests itself not only in the manic desire to please but also in the faux cynicism that swears off relationships altogether. That's really nothing more than a cover-up for the original fear of being hurt and rejected. Whether we are in a relationship or not, one way or another, our fear of being alone can restrict us from *receiving* love.

THE COSTS

So we've had our feminist revolution, we've won many battles in the workforce, but when it comes to relationships, we're back in the retro days of scheming to attract a man and then sublimating our own needs to keep him happy. Here we are in the twenty-first century, following *The Rules* so we can snare that guy who's going to take care of us in a 1950s-style domestic paradise in which happiness is always just around the corner and disaster is one argument away. "The feminist revolution," Maureen Dowd writes in the *New York Times Magazine,* "would have the unexpected consequence of intensifying the confusion between the sexes, leaving women in a tangle of dependence and independence as they entered the 21st century."

Our ultimate confusion is believing that because the salvation of mankind is indeed through love, our lovers are our saviors. "We may give our human loves the unconditional allegiance which we owe only to God," C. S. Lewis warned. "Then they become gods: then they become demons." So great becomes the fear of losing what we have that many of us rush back to hide under the temporary shelter of convention rather than follow the path of self-discovery wherever it might lead. Given adequate time and sufficient fear, we may hide so long that we hardly notice we're slowly suffocating.

If the fear of being alone or abandoned causes us to feverishly pursue a relationship or cling to one, then we are operating solely in a protective mode and we have in effect declared ourselves among the walking dead. We exist, we breathe, we work, but we have shut down the possibilities of a full life.

ON BECOMING FEARLESS IN RELATIONSHIPS
The bottom line is that you can't be in a fearless, fulfilling relationship and be looking over your shoulder for approval at the same time. You've got to choose. If what's most important to you is being regularly patted on the back for good behavior or avoiding punishment for bad behavior (such infractions as too much independence), you'll never be able to reveal your true self in this most intimate of all relationships. Indeed, you won't even know what true self there is to reveal.

To truly love another, to truly overcome our fears, there is no alternative but learning to accept ourselves with all our shortcomings. As long as the expectation continues that relationships will fill our emptiness and insulate us from anxiety and loneliness, we will keep trying to find in them the feelings of safety and contentment we had or longed for in childhood — and we will keep finding disappointment instead. To be truly fearless in relationships, we have to turn off the voices of both our inner critics and society.

"After my first marriage ended, besides feeling fat and old, I feared that I would never find anyone to love me again," Liz Perle, an author and editor, told me. "My ex had fallen in love with a younger, thinner woman who didn't want kids, as I had, and who devoted herself solely to him. Here I was, a middle-aged mom who wanted nothing more than a family. I had been rejected on every level that defined who I was — my body, my independence, my dreams. Needless to say, I was somewhat terrified about being alone for the rest of my life.

"But then one day, a friend urged me to try online dating. After I made merciless fun of it, I decided to try anyway. The anonymous nature of the questionnaire let me portray myself as exactly who I was. I figured that if someone rejected me, at least they wouldn't know my name. So I drew a pretty honest portrait of myself — I only shaved a few pounds off my weight. I put down all my opinions, likes, dislikes, and deal-breakers. The exercise made me realize how much I liked myself — warts and all. As I told a friend, 'Hey, I'd date me.' I figured that if I was going to be involved with someone again, they'd better know exactly what they were getting into.

"To make a long story short, I met a man who loved what I loved about me and who found the rest endearing — or at least tolerable. But if I hadn't been accepting of who I was, I never would have found love again. I would have, instead, tried to twist myself into the shape I thought someone else could love. This is so much easier and much, much stronger than any love I have had before. And we've been married five years now."

It's not just our own self-censors that need to be silenced. The fear of society's censure is a powerful one, as Rachel Jayne, director of customer service for Sportsworld International and mother of three, discovered. "After my twenty-one-year marriage to John ended," she told me, "I was really unhappy and kept evading the question of what I wanted next. Finally, I sat down and drew up an expanded vision with fifty qualities of exactly what I wanted in a relationship. But not things like blue eyes, brown hair, et cetera — more the type of experience I wanted to have. Like I want to feel valued, I want us to have the same goals, and I want our bodies to fit well together. I still have the list, and one day I was with a friend of mine and I read it to her and she flipped out and said, 'You wrote that before you met Justin? Because that's exactly what you have.' And I said I know it.

"I was fifty-three when I met Justin, and he was twenty-four. We both had to overcome what society would think. But given the choice of having society look at me a certain way and having a level of fulfillment and loving beyond anything I could have imagined, I wasn't willing to sacrifice that anymore. It's like you reach a certain age where it just doesn't fricking matter what other people think because at the end of the day I'm the one that has to go to bed with myself.

"We've been together for two years and are enjoying the adventure of being married for the last six months. This doesn't mean we don't have our challenges. The key for us is choosing to be true to ourselves and to return to the loving."

No one bats an eyelash when a man is with a woman twenty or even thirty years younger (and if a comment is offered, it's usually to congratulate the guy). But if a woman is with a younger man, the assumption — wink, wink, nudge, nudge — is that (a) it must be all about sex, (b) it's temporary — not "real," or (c) there is something wrong with the man, the woman, or both.

So for the modern woman, this is a taboo that triggers the primal fear of being shunned by the tribe. And for every woman who goes ahead and dates a younger man, or for that matter someone of another race or a different social class — or another woman — someone, in other words, who doesn't fit the world's idea of an appropriate partner, there is probably at least one other woman who denies herself that love for fear of reprobation.

When we learn to accept ourselves — not just our public achievements and private successes but also our failures, inadequacies, cowardices, and desires — then we can transcend our fears. We master our fears by embracing them, not by subduing them.

Our most meaningful relationships are based on a longing for expansion rather than a preoccupation with comfort and security. To live exuberantly — to fully know and be fully known by another — we must be prepared to illuminate the dark spots in our most intimate relationships and in our selves.

THE GIFT OF FEAR

Mastering our emotions is a matter of recognizing what our gut is really telling us and knowing when to overrule it and when to heed it. Some fears, it turns out, are real and need to be heeded. It helps if we understand something about brain chemistry. In *The Female Brain*, Louann Brizendine examines research showing that the brain of a woman in the throes of falling in love is in a special state fueled by hormones and neurochemicals, particularly oxytocin and dopamine. And when we hug or kiss or touch, more oxytocin is released, "triggering the brain's trust circuits." These hormones can cloud our judgment and flip an inner switch, turning off the brain circuitry that tells us to take things slowly. Good-bye, independence; hello, infatuation.

So at the very moment when fear could be useful in making us more vigilant, the pheromones urge us to rush. Later, when we're already deep into the relationship, we allow the voices we stifled in the beginning to speak — sometimes to scream — that something is very wrong. How often do we hear women say, "He changed"? He "suddenly" became violent, or jealous, or controlling, or distant, or aloof. There was "another woman I didn't know existed." And on and on.

But did he actually change, or did we fail to listen to what world-renowned security consultant Gavin de Becker calls "the gift of fear" and what it was trying to tell us — to slow down and gather information before we rushed into an intimacy that had no foundation? That's where our survival instinct could have been very helpful, allowing us to spend less time, energy, and heartache on all the wrong relationships.

But if we do rush in and make a bad decision — as no doubt we will — let's at least quickly forgive ourselves, learn, and move on.

FAITH IN THE FACE OF FEAR

When things do go wrong, terribly wrong, we question everything — especially ourselves. How could we not have seen infidelity? Where were we inadequate? These questions bring up all the elemental fears I've been discussing. But sometimes, if we think the relationship is worth it, we have to push through our fears and walk through the darkest parts of both ourselves and those we love.

Therapist Heide Banks believes faith in love itself can heal, if we give ourselves time: "Being fearless in love is being willing to open your heart just one more time and recapture the type of innocence we associate with first love.

"I had to face this in my own life — learning to trust again. A terrible breakup left me devastated. It wasn't the being alone part that devastated me; I had spent many years on my own and loved it. It was the loss of innocence and openness. I no longer believed in love. I sought counsel, threw myself into my work, and dated. But something was lost — something I longed to have — a trust that I could love again.

"It is said that the loss of a relationship is the dark night of the soul, but I don't believe it. The real dark night of the soul is not the incident that knocks us into our darkness or the pain that follows. It's in fact the months and years we spend trying to trust again and open our hearts to both life and another individual.

"Four years later, I met the man who was to become my husband, but I still wasn't ready to trust again. I let him know this, and we took the plunge together. To this day I still struggle with trust, and there are days when my mind is running at full speed telling me this will never work out. But it is my commitment to having an open heart that gets me through those days and helps me walk through my fears."

BECOMING ASSERTIVE IN LOVE

One of the things women find hard to do in relationships is make clear what we want. In fact, we fear that doing so might be a turnoff to the man. But part of fearlessness is expressing what's important to us and knowing that we are strong enough — and willing — to walk away if the other person can't handle the mere expression of our needs.

Of course, we should also be aware of *how* we ask for what we want. Are we asking or demanding? Is what we're asking for what we really want or a stand-in for something else that we're actually too afraid to bring up? And if we don't always get what we want (which is inevitable), are we going to be bitter and resentful about it?

One key to getting past the fear of being assertive in love is to recognize that conflict is not only normal in our intimate relationships but can actually strengthen them. According to Diane Sollee, director of the Coalition for Marriage, Family and Couples Education, "The number one predictor of divorce is the habitual avoidance of conflict. We often avoid conflict precisely because we are so much in love, and we believe disagreeing or fighting might cause a divorce. But the way to have a happy marriage is to learn how to handle the inevitable disagreements that are part of every relationship."

When we hide from conflict, we're avoiding a chance to deepen our relationships. I remember a beautiful sermon I heard years ago on "becoming married." It was given by the then dean of the Houston Cathedral, Pittman McGehee. He urged us to see marriage as a process and, especially, to be open to the negative side of intimacy — the hurt, the criticisms, the losses that bring depth to the relationship and bring us closer to each other. He cautioned us to be wary of a relationship that has no room for anger or pain, that is lived on the surface of niceness behind smiling masks that block us from experiencing our own vulnerability and each other's reality. He pleaded with us to realize that the self-protective devices behind which we barricade ourselves are actually self-destructive.

By conflict I don't, of course, mean physical danger. That's when running away is the only option. Leslie Morgan Steiner, editor of *Mommy Wars: Stay-at-Home and Career Moms Face Off* on *Their Choices, Their Lives, Their Families,* left her abusive husband at twenty-six: "I did what I had to, to protect myself. I erased what pride I had left and recruited the forces of friends and strangers. For months I slept with a dresser blocking my bedroom door, the phone on my pillow. I relocated to a city hundreds of miles away. It's been fifteen years in this second lifetime of mine. I'm grateful for every second."

THE REWARDS OF THE REAL THING

The rewards of emotional fearlessness — the willingness to show anger, love, even fear — are many. The deepest of these is the gift of a profound intimacy, captured by Tom Stoppard in his play *The Real Thing:* "It's to do with knowing and being known. I remember how it stopped seeming odd that in biblical Greek knowing was used for making love. Whosit knew so-and-so. Carnal knowledge. It's what lovers trust each other with, knowledge of each other, not of the flesh but through the flesh, knowledge of self, the real him, the real her, in extremis, the mask slipped from the face. Every other version of oneself is on offer to the public. . . . But in pairs we insist that we give ourselves to each other. What selves? What's left? What else is there that hasn't been dealt out like playing cards? A sort of knowledge. Personal, final, uncompromised. Knowing, being known. I revere that."

Knowing and letting oneself be known require overcoming many ancient fears — but it's worth every risk.

It's also a never-ending process. Cheryl Saban, now in her third — and very happy — marriage, commented, "The fear I sometimes have is how to make sure the love stays. But then, I know the answer. . . . You encourage it, you nurture it, you caress it, you build it, you protect it, you honor it, and you continue to grow it!"

Kathy Freston, author of *The One: Finding Soul Mate Love and Making It Last,* says the clearest sign you're in the right relationship is that "you like who you're becoming when you're with this person." So in the end, it's all about finding your best self, not losing yourself in another. About finding someone you like yourself with, not someone to save you from yourself. I love how this notion takes the idea of finding "the one" out of the fairy-tale land of Prince Charming sweeping us off our feet and puts the onus squarely on us. How contrary to the traditional notions of romantic love involving the idea that we'll be "swept away," "knocked off our feet," or "fall head over heels" — not exactly healthy states of being! I much prefer the kind of love that comes down to "I like me best when I'm with you — fearless and at peace."

FEARLESS SINGLEHOOD

I've been single, I've been married, and I've been divorced. And although my own marriage didn't work, and my parents' marriage didn't work, I'm blessed to have good friends in happy, long-term marriages. So, even though I'm not putting on a ring anytime soon, I'm by no means a cynic about marriage. But I have also seen way too many marriages held together by nothing but fear and convention — relationships that are all anchor and no sail.

"Ships in the harbor are safe," someone once said, "but this is not what ships are made for." And sometimes relationships become not partnerships in life's great adventure but excuses to stop ourselves from growing, taking risks, and living life to the fullest. The presence of children, of course, always complicates the decision whether to stay together or move on, but what matters most is that whatever the decision, it comes from fearlessness and not from fear.

Many divorced women I know have told me what a relief it was to leave their unfulfilling marriages and how comfortable they've become with being on their own. "I'm at a place in my life," writer Carol Hoenig reports, "where I don't believe I will ever remarry. And I'm okay with that. After having been married for close to twenty years and raising three children, I told my husband that the marriage was over. This was one of the bravest decisions I'd made up to that point." Carol now has her hands full with blogging and writing novels. She's still open to the possibility of a relationship but much wiser: "I have learned that if I do find a man who sweeps me off my feet again, I'll land where I want to without losing my balance. Self-esteem does that."

And there are young women, too, embracing going solo as a virtue in itself, and not just as a way station before marriage. As Lisa Ling, former cohost of *The View* and now globe-trotting host of National Geographic's *Explorer,* writes: "When I was a child I had no doubt in my mind that by thirty I would have the 'ideal American life' — a wonderful husband, two kids, and a beautiful home complete with white picket fence. I'm thirty-two years old right now, am still single, and, quite frankly, the idea of getting married and having children is simply not even on my radar. I absolutely love what I do and the lifestyle I lead. . . . I am deeply grateful that I grew up in a totally nontraditional Asian family. It has enabled me to embrace the fact that it's okay to lead an unconventional life. At this point I feel, 'Why should I start living a conventional life now?' "

Marja Adriance, who runs my office, came up with a dozen reasons why it can be great to be on your own:

1. Because I can talk to myself out loud. And not just a little bit but whole rambling conversations where I take both sides, reprimand myself, take it back, offer advice, ignore it, recount old stories, crack myself up, delight, enlighten, and inspire. I am my own best friend.

2. Because I can go all day long without getting dressed or brushing my teeth and no one cares.

3. Because, with no one watching, I am a really good dancer.

4. Because I can eat the last cookie without asking if anyone else wants it.

5. Because I can scrub the entire bathroom floor with a very small tile brush at 1:00 a.m. when I'm sick of looking at it.

6. Because I fall in love every day with my amazing friends, none of whom are hanging out with me only because I'm having sex with them.

7. Because I can just be quiet and not have to worry about being rude or boring.
8. Because I don't have to think for even a moment about what anyone else wants to do.
9. Because no one ever wrote their manifesto at a party.
10. Because after I've spent many hours alone, restless and bored, wondering where I went wrong in my life, inspiration (often) comes.
11. Because I get the *whole* bed.
12. Because I'm released from the poisonous snare of comparison and I am smart enough, pretty enough, charming enough, talented enough, accomplished enough, educated enough, kind enough, funny enough, interesting enough, good enough!

Marja is also fearless enough. She's not ruling out getting married, but she's perfectly content being single. Whether we are single or in a relationship, the most important thing is to approach our lives not out of lack and need but with fearlessness and trust.

Diane Keaton on fearlessness

——•◆•——

HAVING JUST CELEBRATED a "milestone birthday," here is my biggest take-away after sixty years on the planet: There is great value in being fearless. For too much of my life, I was too afraid, too frightened by it all. That fear is one of my biggest regrets. I wish I had put myself out there a little bit more and experienced people more instead of protecting myself.

I spent a lot of time protecting myself. I mean, I've met a lot of extraordinary people over the years — and I just wish I had been able to open myself up to them more.

I remember when I was filming *Godfather III.* My father was diagnosed with an inoperable brain tumor, and I flew home. He told me, "I only wish I'd done more. I wish I had worked less at something I didn't really enjoy." I've been blessed to work at something I love, but I wish his words had emboldened me more.

I've spent a lot of my life worrying — especially when I was younger. I used to listen to Judy Garland all the time — I love Judy Garland and her music. But I started to realize that if you keep singing like that, singing songs of being victimized by love over and over and over again, it can't help but have a profound effect on your life. At a certain point, you're programming yourself to become a victim of love. And I decided that that wasn't for me, so I forged ahead. And I feel as if I've managed to avoid becoming a victim of that particular kind of love.

A sense of freedom is something that, happily, comes with age and life experience. In *The Second Sex,* Simone de Beauvoir says that as they approach fifty, a lot of women are set free from the anxiety and the mortification and the humiliation of intimate relationships with men — the opposite sex. For some reason, you are suddenly free from it. And thank God for that.

It's the upside of sticking around this long.

Diane Keaton is on the board of directors at the Los Angeles Conservancy.

Fearless in Parenting

Beyond the Guilted Age

THERE IS NO love more intense than the love we have for our children. And wherever you find intense love, you're sure to find intense fear lurking just beneath the surface.

The ease with which love can suddenly flip into fear has not exactly made parenting any easier in the modern era. The urge to protect our offspring is primal. In an age of kidnappings, AIDS, drugs, school violence, hypersexuality, not to mention terrorism and the bird flu, all of our traditional fears about our children's safety and well-being are multiplied and magnified.

My daughter Isabella was eleven years old when she started being obsessively careful about what she ate. She settled on protein, vegetables, and a little fruit, and that was all.

Gone were the carbs, gone were the sweets. And in came things like waking up earlier and earlier and jumping rope for long periods of time or getting me out of bed for a long, fast walk in our neighborhood before school. It was when — at her twelfth birthday party, with all her best friends around the table — she didn't touch her birthday cake that I realized we had a serious problem. In retrospect, I should have realized it much sooner, but because she had always been rail-thin and athletic, and because she was eating the way I like to eat, I just missed the signals.

As soon as I realized that we were dealing with early symptoms of anorexia, I arranged to see a doctor, who basically told Isabella that if she didn't put on ten pounds over the next two months she would be hospitalized. I don't know who was more afraid — Isabella or me. My mother had been dead for two years, but my first thought was, What would my mother think? What would Isabella's grandmother — for whom food was a sacred part of life — think of her granddaughter's rejection of it?

My fears were also mixed up with guilt. Was this my fault? Did it have to do with the fact that I was also rejecting food to control my weight? Was I subliminally reinforcing in my daughter the destructive messages about thinness that pervade our culture?

We were lucky — Isabella quickly started putting on weight and (knock on carbs) seems to have put any anorexic tendencies behind her. But I still remember as though it were yesterday a day when the children and I were in London on vacation a couple of months after the visit with the doctor. Isabella was getting her hair washed at a small hairdressing shop near the hotel. I looked in the sink and saw that it was filled with chunks of her hair. The sight of Isabella's beautiful red hair lying lifeless in the sink filled me with terror. I rushed back to the hotel and called the doctor, who explained that hair loss is often a delayed reaction to weight loss. My fear subsided, but that night I couldn't help but fixate on every bite Isabella consumed at dinner.

FEAR OF CHILDBIRTH

The miracle of birth has, for all our scientific knowledge about it, never been diminished over the centuries. The staggering reality that we mortals can accomplish the act of human creation — matching in some sense God's creation on the sixth day of his labors — leaves us changed forever. But the prospect of childbirth can also leave us paralyzed with fear.

I lost my first baby five months into my pregnancy. As a result, I spent my next pregnancy utterly terrified. So much so that even though I was thirty-eight, I refused to have amniocentesis because it carried a tiny risk of miscarriage. Instead, I simply prayed that my baby would be healthy. I was absolutely convinced that it was a girl, hence all the pink clothes and lilac in the nursery. "How do you know?" my husband would ask. "I know," I would reply.

I was planning a natural childbirth and working with a wonderful midwife who helped calm my fears considerably, but we'd also made arrangements for the delivery to take place at UCLA Hospital — just in case there were any last-minute complications. So, ten days before my due date, we moved from Santa Barbara, where we were living at the time, to a hotel near UCLA. The idea was that I would go through as much of the labor as possible at the hotel and then we'd just scoot on over to UCLA for the delivery. A fine plan, agreed to by all concerned.

Except the baby. We moved into the appointed hotel room at the appointed hour and waited the predicted ten days. Nothing. Fifteen days. Nothing. Twenty. Twenty-five. Not a thing. My fears were mounting. Meanwhile, the hotel had been sold to

Japanese investors, creating a media flap over the price and foreign ownership of another piece of prized California property.

On the thirtieth day of our sojourn at the hotel, there was at last some stirring of interest on the part of the baby. Within an hour, it was more than casual interest; I was unmistakably in labor. To manage the pain, the midwife and I started taking walks around the grounds, past the herb garden, across the grass, and back toward the lobby.

By now, however, journalists and photographers from both Japan and America had descended on the hotel to cover the growing ownership fracas. So our strolls were punctuated by my occasional sharp intakes of breath, the midwife's quiet and confident words of support, and the stares of worried disbelief from tourists, Japanese cameramen, and a couple of local television crews. When, according to the midwife, I was within an hour of delivering, Michael piled all of us — by then my mother and sister had joined us — into the car, and we were off to the hospital. Thirty minutes later Christina was born, and my fear of childbirth was finally dissolved.

Lynda Obst, producer of *Sleepless in Seattle, Contact,* and *How to Lose a Guy in 10 Days,* among other movies, ended up having a C-section without her husband even being allowed in the room. "Women are funny about fear," she told me. "We want to be held and cuddled and told everything is going to be all right. We want to be babied. But this is the last thing we need when we face our most difficult moments. We need to buck up and learn what men have learned on the playing fields of sport. The pep talk we hear must come from inside ourselves. The holding arms must be our own.

"So, right before my cesarean section, as my pulse quickened and my mouth went dry and they sliced open my belly, I slowed down my breath and repeated my mantra: 'When the going gets tough, the tough get going.' Everything is survivable, except death. And even that we have no choice but to both fight fearlessly and accept graciously."

Even breast-feeding provokes primal fears. What if my milk doesn't come? What if it isn't enough for my baby to survive? And even if your milk is plentiful and you've mastered the art of pumping, "breastophobia" is so rampant in America that more than twenty states have had to pass legislation just to clarify that women have the right to breast-feed in public — that breast-feeding is not a criminal offense like indecent exposure. In California, the bill, which passed in 1997, was actually opposed by fourteen legislators. And no, they were not all male. Assemblywoman Lynne Leach explained that she objected to breast-feeding in public places, especially where children were present. Oh dear, and I thought it was breast-feeding *without* a child present that was inappropriate in public.

So here in this nation founded by English Puritans, women have been asked to leave stores, museums, restaurants, health clubs — including the women-only sections of gyms — because they were brazen enough to feed their hungry babies. Even this very natural act can fill us with fear.

BUBBLE-WRAPPING OUR KIDS

The dangers that threaten our children grow as our babies grow. No wonder sales of high-tech surveillance systems are booming —

satellite-linked stuffed animals, ID-encoded clothing, devices to connect children's cell phones to global-positioning satellites, even full-scale video monitoring of their rooms from wherever you are. The issue of warrantless spying may be up for debate in Washington, but in the home it has been settled.

This isn't an entirely unreasonable response to the world our kids inhabit, but there is no faster way to make the joy of parenting — and hence the quality of our parenting — plummet than by going overboard with overprotection.

Novelist Leslie Lehr sums up the real dangers our children face: "A schoolmate of my daughter's blew his brains out last year. Another overdosed. Another got pregnant. These are just the ones I know about. In a large public school, these statistics aren't high, but they are always devastating. In a culture of sex, drugs, and academic pressure, how do we protect our children? Maybe I was lucky to come out of adolescence unscathed, but how could I guarantee that my daughters would? According to the experts, every child is at risk.

"So I spouted statistics, warned them about weakness, and fretted at the first sign of tears. We practiced what to say if someone offered drugs and how to call me from anywhere, anytime. I had no reason to search their drawers, but I read every shredded note that I found in the laundry. I called parents before playdates to ask if there were guns in the house. Call me paranoid, but call me within five minutes of curfew. My girls knew I trusted them; I just didn't trust anyone else. And for a while, it worked. Both girls were 'straight edge.' Yet there was one risk I hadn't considered: Fear was ruining our relationship."

And hovering over all our loving and protecting is the fear

that our children will disconnect from us, even reject us —
especially in adolescence.

Therapist Fran Lasker and I met through our daughters, who
go to the same school. She describes the problem well: "We are
bringing our children up in an age that strives to empower them.
While this is a wonderful thing, there are obvious pitfalls. My
sixteen-year-old daughter considers *me* lucky that she 'talks' to
me. There is a veiled threat that she will in fact cut off communication if I don't toe the line regarding the extension of privileges
to her. She thinks that when she tells me she plans to drink alcohol at a party, her communication of this gives her a green light.
I'm so hungry for this openness that I have to fight the tempta-
tion to grant the green light."

We live in such fear of the pull drugs, sex, and our children's
peers have over our kids that we are desperate to keep them close
to us, even at the cost of turning parenting into a one-sided
friendship.

THE MYTH OF THE SUPERMOM

Our fears about our children's safety become mixed up with our
fears about our worth as parents. The fear of failing as a parent
confronts us not just when we have to deal with real crises —
drugs, eating disorders, unwanted pregnancy — but even when
facing the most trivial situations.

As columnist Bill Lohmann writes in the *Richmond Times-
Dispatch:* "You send your daughter off to preschool with her dress
on backwards, you show up late to pick up your child at the bus
stop, you forget to give your kids their Sunday school offering, or
you lose your temper and go into your Bobby Knight act. It can

be awfully frustrating when you mess up. No matter how tiny the gaffe, no matter how honest the mistake. All of the good work seems somehow blemished. It still gnaws at you after you have forgotten, fumed, or failed in some way as a parent."

I'm convinced that once you become a mother — whether you stay at home or work — when they take the baby out, they put the guilt in. From that moment, both baby and guilt start growing. And as our children grow up, the fear that we're never good enough, that we're never doing enough, only becomes more intense.

Compounding the guilt every mother feels is the social expectation for us to be not just good, caring mothers but absolute supermoms, whether or not we work outside the home. Susan Douglas, coauthor of *The Mommy Myth: The Idealization of Motherhood and How It Undermines Women*, puts it this way: "We're supposed to pipe Mozart into our wombs so our babies come out perfectly tuned . . . drill them with flashcards when they're six months old . . . drive them ten hours round-trip to a soccer match, build a fun house for them in the backyard . . . and paint it beautifully. And home-school them and, of course, by the way, look sexy."

Where do these demands originate? Judith Warner, author of *Perfect Madness: Motherhood in the Age of Anxiety*, blames both the media's fantasy-generating machine and our own fears of measuring up. "We live in a time where there is an enormous gap between the wealthy and everyone else," she says. "Where life has become very, very competitive and very expensive, and where the basic things of a good middle-class life, access to good education for your children, the ability to buy a house in a nice neighborhood, the ability to get good health care and be able to pay for it . . . have become almost luxuries, and people want to be sure that their kids can compete and be successful and have a solid middle-class life in the future."

Warner also points out that the concern isn't just for our children's best interests but can also stem from a misplaced desire to control the outside world. "The desperate, grasping, and controlling way so many women go about the job of motherhood," she writes, "turning energy that used to demand social change inward into control-freakishness, is our hallmark as a generation. We have taken it upon ourselves as super mothers to be everything to our children that society refuses to be: not just loving nurturers but educators, entertainers, guardians of environmental purity, protectors of a stable and prosperous future."

WORKING-MOTHER ANGST

As women are increasingly juggling motherhood with careers, they are compounding their feelings of guilt with soul-destroying fears about abandoning their children to strangers — babysitters, day-care providers, and teachers.

Leslie Morgan Steiner underscores how tough this can be: "Three times, three babies, I walked away from a newborn tucked in a stranger's arms after maternity leave passed. The permanent and conflicting emotions I felt still flicker in slow motion on the camera of my heart."

And on the camera of my heart, too. I remember being at a dinner in New York while my daughters, then seven and nine, were at home in Los Angeles. I was, as always when I'm away from them, wearing my two-time-zone watch (and observing my internal time clock as well). I glanced at my watch and knew that at that very instant Isabella was just back from a playdate and Christina was in the middle of her homework. A friend of mine, also a working mother, arrived late and announced that she had just come from a function at her daughter's school. "Actually," she whispered in my ear, "there was no school function. I just wanted to put her to bed without rushing. But it's so hard for people to understand that." I certainly understood — and the guilt that started to well up spoiled the rest of the dinner for me.

On top of all this, we're at a cultural moment when there is more sympathy for the juggling act of the engaged father (look at that guy with his briefcase and his Baby Björn — what a mensch!) than for that of the working mother or even her stay-at-home counterpart. We fear that even asking for any adjustments to be made for us at work will somehow threaten our hard-won economic advancements and relegate us back to the "mommy track." So while there are few things for which a man gets more social approval than leaving a business meeting early to go to his daughter's soccer game, a working mother, worried about the mommy track stigma, will either miss the game or theatrically apologize for leaving. More likely, she'll overcompensate and choose work, or use subterfuge when choosing the children, as my friend at the dinner party did.

AT-HOME AMBIVALENCE

Stay-at-home moms are burdened with their own set of fears. The combination of isolation and a loss of professional identity can easily leave them struggling with fear, desperately trying to figure out whether they are adequate parents, especially when parenting full-time doesn't turn out to be what they imagined.

Huffington Post reader Lori Lenzer comments: "I became a first-time mom at age thirty-eight after working full-time for fourteen years. I now stay at home with my daughter. I have found that the guilt aspect of parenting tends to become more intense if you allow the thoughtless comments of others to permeate your own sense of self-worth. There are the people who act like 'Oh! How easy it must be to be a mom!' Never mind that I didn't get a complete night's sleep for over eight months . . . that I had episodes where I was up for twenty-four hours straight . . . that I did not have a hot meal for months . . . that I could not always go to the bathroom when I really wanted to! When your child is born, his or her needs come first . . . period."

Then, too, there's the fear that life outside is passing us by. Whatever choice we've made, or life has made for us, can seem like the wrong one.

D-I-V-O-R-C-E

Whether we work or stay at home, fear often increases exponentially when we are, or become, single mothers — coping alone, helping our kids deal with the stresses of divorce, or sharing parenting tasks with someone with whom we no longer see eye-to-eye.

I married late and I married for life. So when, after eleven years, it was clear that my marriage was over, I was filled with one overwhelming fear above all others: What would I tell my children? How could I — who would do anything to shield them from pain — be the one to actually inflict on them such a real and possibly lasting wound?

Christina was eight and Isabella was six. Isabella, to my surprise and relief, took the news in stride. But Christina was devastated. She steadfastly refused to accept it and kept pleading with me every day to go out to dinner with Daddy. I'm not sure if that was the influence of the movie *The Parent Trap,* but she had convinced herself that a romantic candlelit dinner would solve all her parents' problems. After all, if she loved both her parents so much, how could they not love each other?

We moved from Washington to Los Angeles a few days before my divorce became final in 1997. Christina had a new house. She soon had a new school and new friends, but I could see she wasn't giving up the hope that her dad and I would get together again. I lost count of how many times she watched that movie!

But I couldn't allow my fears about the consequences of my divorce to cripple me as a mother. I had a clear choice to make: spending my energies fearing the future or doing the best I could for my children in the present.

THE COURAGE TO BE A SINGLE MOTHER

And what of the woman who decides to have a child without being married and having no partner? Although she faces the same fears all mothers face, the lack of anyone to depend on emotionally, physically, and financially can greatly intensify her anxiety level. And she has to face the social stigma that still accompanies such a decision. For Julia Mays, formerly a senior executive in the entertainment industry and for the moment a full-time mom, the choice to pursue motherhood as a single woman meant that she had to confront two sets of fears: the fear of not being up to the challenge of single parenting and the fear of disapproval from those around her: "My parents had loving expectations for me from the time my mother held me in her arms and my father pushed my stroller. They saw me married to a good man with little ones at my feet and grandkids with two parents. My choice to conceive on my own meant the destruction of their hopes for me."

Many families have no frame of reference into which to put a decision like Julia's. "But once they start whispering their terrible family secret to a few others," Julia says, "they'll begin to discover that just about everyone knows someone who had a baby using artificial intervention, using a donor, or through adoption. In my case, my mother, who was at first so disappointed in my choice, was nonetheless present during my egg retrieval and return. She now brags that she was present at the conception . . . to her church friends!

"My mother has gone from fear and disgust to a bewildered kind of pride in me. My fearlessness in the face of the unthinkable has opened doors to her that never would have opened otherwise, and she's starting to see herself as having choices, too."

Holly Vanderhaar, a graduate student, also chose single motherhood. This is not to say she made the decision lightly: "Ask any of my childhood friends: I have always wanted to be a mother. Throughout all the twists and rambles that my professional aspirations have taken, it has been my one constant, the center around which my aimless life has drifted."

When Holly discovered that she had conceived identical twins, "doubt crept hand in hand with pregnancy hormones into the equation. The balance of power had shifted. I was going to be outnumbered. I can handle one, but how am I going to handle two? At once? That was not part of my game plan.

"Now my daughters are three years old, bold and audacious, dauntless, optimistic. Every situation is an opportunity for excitement and adventure. It never crosses their minds that danger lurks, that they might fail or get hurt or be disappointed. God, I want so badly to bottle that and give it back to them in ten years, in case the world seems as bleak to them as it did to me at thirteen."

But that has not been the end of Holly's fear: "I worry about the world and its intolerance, especially in our politically and religiously conservative suburb. I'm troubled by the thought that someone, someday will make them feel 'less' because they are donor-conceived. I hope they will have the courage to stand up for themselves and their convictions in any company, but they shouldn't have to pay the price for a life I chose for them. I'm fiercely proud of my decision to become a single mother, but I gave birth to girls, not battle flags, and I'm not raising them to be the foot soldiers in my personal battle."

With all the fears and worries, this is Holly's bottom line: "Before having my girls, I was adrift. Now I'm simultaneously anchored and set aloft."

ON BECOMING A FEARLESS MOTHER

Motherhood brings out reserves of courage we never knew we had. Huffington Post commenter Deborah Daniels Wood writes: "Being a mom is probably the one thing that will make most women fearless. We would gladly step in front of a speeding train, a bullet, a raging mad dog, whatever it was that was threatening our children."

That's how I got through Isabella's eating issues. What helped me at the time, and has always helped me in dealing with my fears, is that I have to be fearless for them, because there is nothing that strikes fear in a child's heart faster than a fearful parent. Knowing that you have to at least appear fearless for your children — to convey the assurance that everything is going to be all right — can have the effect of actually making you fearless.

Huffington Post reader Lia Hadley sent me an e-mail about a trip she took to London with her then nine-year-old daughter: "When we arrived at the airport, it was late in the evening, and we had to take a long train ride into the center of the city. As we were waiting for the train (with not another child in sight), my daughter began to cry because it was all so strange, there were so many people, and it was dark and way past her bedtime. Trying to show her that she didn't have to worry because, hey, she was with her mom and a world traveler to boot, we had a discussion, which at least calmed her to the point that she stopped crying. By the end of the journey (five days later), she had had such a good time that she said she wanted to move to London when she grew up."

Some time later, Lia asked her daughter what had changed the London adventure from being scary to being fun. "I think," she said, "it was because I realized that despite the fact that you got lost all the time, we always managed to get to where we wanted to go. You would ask all sorts of strangers for directions, and the people were so friendly and so helpful, and we had such interesting conversations, that I realized being lost can be a lot of fun."

When I look back at my own childhood, my mother looms large as a teacher of fearlessness. Some of the ways she taught fearlessness to my sister and me were more eccentric than others.

One night when my sister and I were in our teens, we were on our way to see Chekhov's *Three Sisters*. We walked out of the house, closing the door behind us. My mother immediately realized that she'd forgotten her purse inside — the purse containing not only the tickets to the show and her money but the key to the house. Any normal person would probably have rearranged the night's priorities, canceling the theater and getting a locksmith to open the door.

Not my mother. She didn't blink an eye. She went to the superintendent's apartment, knocked on the door, and asked him for some cash. We all climbed into a taxi, and when we arrived at the theater, she went up to the box office and explained what had happened.

They had us wait until everyone had been seated, and then they gave us three empty seats. My sister, Agapi, and I kept asking how we were going to get back into the house, to which my mother would say, "Don't think about it, just enjoy the play [which we did, by the way], and it will all work out."

It so happened that our apartment in Athens was on the third floor, opposite the fire station. My mother had a plan. When we got home, she went over to the firehouse and, in her charming way, asked the firemen if they could please bring a ladder over to a window of our apartment. Which they did. In short order, the window was open and we were in the house. Of course, my mother then served them soup, and we all had a great time!

I remember that night whenever I'm faced with canceled flights, lost wallets, and plans gone awry. My mother was a master at not ever panicking and trusting life to always give her solutions. She preferred to live in the moment — even if that moment was one in which she was not in possession of the keys to her apartment — with the assurance that it would all work out. The ability to trust is an amazing quality, and it was deep in her DNA. That trust and lack of fear paid her back well, keeping her open and receptive to solutions.

For Diane von Furstenberg, the most powerful lessons in fearlessness also came from her mother. Diane took the fashion industry by storm in the seventies when she designed a little wrap dress that launched a billion-dollar business. Thirty years and many ventures later, she still credits her mother. "My mother," she told me, "always said that fear is not an option. When I was eight years old she put me on a train from Brussels to Paris on my own. I was very afraid, but I was also proud to arrive safely at my destination. My mother was a Holocaust survivor, and when she was freed from the concentration camp by the Russians in 1945, she weighed forty-nine pounds. It took me a very long time to realize the enormity of what she had been through and of my heritage — and the way she had been able to turn such pain into something positive. I grew up with a legacy that life is a miracle and that I'm the daughter of a survivor, not a victim. So when I'm in pain or in fear, I look through it for the light and the fearlessness."

When there are dead ends there are also U-turns, and if we

don't panic, bridges can appear — we just need to trust that there is a way. And there is *always* a way. That knowledge is a gift of fearlessness we can model for our kids.

NOT ALL FEARS ARE CREATED EQUAL

If courage is the knowledge of what is not to be feared, there is nothing like becoming a mother to help us prioritize and recognize how trivial many of our fears are compared to what really matters.

Janet Grillo, a writer-producer living in Los Angeles whose son has autism, told me: "The biggest fear a mother has is that her child will become damaged. That the perfect wonder of her baby will be undone somehow. That she will turn her head just at the moment he slips. That the spill of scalding coffee, the out-turned handle of a pot, the stray pill, will find her child. I don't know if the vaccines I insisted upon, as a responsible parent following responsible medical advice, caused him harm. Or if the antibiotics prescribed to fight off strep did him in. Or if the toxins in the air and water that pervade everything we eat and breathe crescendoed, after generations, to a breaking point. Or if it was none of this, but maybe my son's genetic destiny, a ticking clock that would strike when he turned two no matter what I did or did not do. Or perhaps my fear itself called it forth, as some sort of extraordinary response from an unkind God.

"What I do know is that when my alert, engaged, charming, and vivacious son turned two, he began, hour by hour, day by day, to drift away. As if by helium, he lifted away from us, from our family, from our world, and inward toward a remote and private place."

It was the hardest and most frightening thing Janet and her

husband, film director David O. Russell, had ever faced. But, Janet told me, "Ultimately, faith and fear could not coexist. One had to eventually prevail out of this eternal pull. I simply did not have the luxury to feel fear. Fear had become, in the face of my child's immediate need, an indulgence. He was here and autism was engulfing him, and I could either reach beyond myself and into the fog that gripped him and pull him out or I could continue fearing that I would lose him. Fear had to fall by the wayside. And faith is what emerged in the tiny triumphs of his returned gaze."

Children clearly help us tap into this faith, the source of the life force that vaporizes fears. They help us see the world in a more trusting way and discover a love we did not know was possible.

WORK ISN'T A DIRTY WORD

I asked *Mommy Wars* editor Leslie Morgan Steiner about her journey from fear to fearlessness. She described continuing to work after having kids as her "second fearless act." (Her first was leaving an abusive husband.)

"I could have stayed home," she said, "dependent on my husband or the government or some other inchoate combination of luck and charity. Some women do, and that's the right decision for them. Instead, I trusted myself. I hoped. I cried. I acted fearless even when I was afraid. I got up and went to work each day. Motherhood was mine. I needed to provide for my children and to take care of myself so I could take care of them."

For me, a greater fearlessness came in part when I accepted that I was never going to give up my work for full-time parenting, and in part when I stopped comparing myself with my own mother, the perfect full-time, nothing-else-matters mom. I now know that every day gives me many opportunities to make choices that cumulatively have a dramatic effect on my children's lives. It's these small everyday decisions — rather than some grand theoretical answers — that will determine whether the balls that drop during our juggling act will be our children. As for me, I've become less afraid that I'm blowing it as a parent. Less afraid that I'm making the wrong choices. Less afraid that every little thing I'm doing wrong or failing to do is somehow causing permanent damage — even though my children may once in a while make claims to the contrary. (Have you noticed what effective guilt-sensing — and guilt-wielding — machines our children can be?)

That said, I've found that I cannot blind myself to the difference it makes in my children's lives — made extremely obvious by the difference in their smiles — when I choose not just "quality time" but uninterrupted quantity time with them (and in reality, they are pretty much the same thing). I'm more important than their peers, and I need to remain more important through their teenage years.

But in the end, as psychotherapist Heide Banks told me: "If you look at the best research on parenting, it comes down to one thing and one thing only. Not what you teach your children or how much time you spend with them, or if you read to them or not. What it comes down to is who you are, because we teach who we are. You read, your child will read. You watch too much TV, your child will. You do service in the world, your child will do service in the world. So the best way to get past all the worries is to be the best you that you can be. And forgive yourself when you are not. And not to hold unrealistic expectations of your children when you are in no way showing them the behavior you demand from them. Be an example to yourself that your child can be proud of."

DEALING WITH DIVORCE

Because about half of all marriages end in divorce, we have to first forgive ourselves and then find innovative ways to minimize the damage of divorce on our children, using love as our guide.

In my case, one thing that was very important to both children was for the four of us to be able to spend Christmas and their birthdays together as a family. So, even though Michael and I have been through many rough patches in the almost ten years since our divorce — his coming out as bisexual two years after our marriage ended, my running for governor, our different views on the children's education — we make a huge effort to work through all the difficulties and get back to being friends, forever tied together by the two children we've brought into the world.

With almost no interruption we've continued to spend every Christmas Day and every birthday together. And by working through the difficult times, we've become closer than ever since our divorce. Indeed, last April — on April 12, to be precise — a magnificent bouquet of flowers that included twenty yellow roses arrived at my home. The card said, "Happy 20th Anniversary. We'll always be the parents of two remarkable young women. Love, Michael." It would have been our twentieth wedding anniversary.

We did not survive as a couple, but at least we've survived in the joint parenting of our two children. And this has made it much easier for me to move to fearlessness about the impact of the divorce on the girls.

Beyond the wounds of divorce and the fears for our children, many women are suddenly faced with the need to make a living when they may be completely ill equipped for that. Nelle Bellamy-Doyle, now eighty years old, retired, and an avid golfer, found herself "at the precipice of total fear," as she puts it, when her marriage ended and she was left with three young children to support. The worst part was when her brother, her only living relative, actually reprimanded her: "Nelle, you're a housewife, a mother. Maybe this divorce wasn't such a smart choice." Her first postdivorce job was at a travel agency, where she shared a desk and was given a quota to meet. Two travel agencies later, she got her own desk. "From that point on, I knew I had a shot, a second chance. This was the beginning, not the end, and for the first time as an adult I felt real fearlessness."

FIND THE COURAGE TO PARENT

Fran Lasker shared with me how, for her, being the parent sometimes means being willing to be the "bad guy" for the greater good. "The notion of choosing your battles is one that we all must live by. I don't think that any child is served by a draconian parent, and it's obviously of paramount importance to have a harmonious relationship with one's child," she told me. "So how does a parent straddle the balance of strength and acquiescence? The battles that should be chosen are an individual's choice. I think that a great deal of parenting is a medley of compromise and deal-making, but there are some situations where being a parent is the only option. If you suspect that your child is doing drugs or drinking alcohol, test them, involve them in doing some research or community service that will help raise their awareness regarding the dangers of what they are doing. If they are damaging themselves in any way, do your best to stand up to them. Although our kids may kick and scream and momentarily loathe us, they will eventually draw closer to a parent who they sense is strong enough to protect them. I think underneath it all children actually do want to be children."

We will always fear for our children in bad times, but the degree of fear diminishes as we do the next right thing, one action at a time. As we keep the goal — healthy, independent children — in sight, we can see how some of our kids' setbacks can actually strengthen them later in life. They want us to protect them, but sometimes courageous mothering means we have to let them make mistakes.

"If you wrap kids up in cotton wool, they don't learn anything," community education worker Raymond Branton observes. "I believe that a little risk is a healthy thing; it's all part of life. You have to remember that the statistics show children are mostly safe when they are out playing. Of course it's a terrible tragedy when something does happen, but you have to remember how many millions of children go out to play every day and are perfectly fine."

We don't just stress about our kids. We stress about comparing ourselves to our own mothers. According to a Pew Research Center poll, 56 percent of women, when asked how they compared with their mothers, gave themselves lower marks. Count me among them. And it's not just our mothers we compare ourselves with, it's also our contemporaries. Novelist Leslie Lehr discovered very dramatically just how meaningless these comparisons are: "One day, when I was shopping for a new coffeemaker, I ran into a mom I knew from the elementary school PTA. I had always admired her beautiful family: their weekly barbecues, the children's tennis skill, and their frequent honor roll status. That morning, her eyes were red and glassy. When I asked if she was all right, she burst into tears. She had just shipped her child off to wilderness camp in Montana. It was a last chance at rehab. If it happened to this good mother, it could happen to anyone. There are forces beyond a parent's control. I realized I needed to stop being afraid of life."

EMBRACE UNCERTAINTY AND IMPERFECTION

One of the greatest ways to become a fearless mother is to give up the idea of doing it perfectly, indeed to embrace uncertainty and imperfection.

Not all decisions we make are obvious. Kimberly Marteau Emerson, president of the Los Angeles Zoo Commission, talked about how fearful she was when she had to make a decision about her ten-year-old daughter's future. Jackie had been offered a contract from Walt Disney Records to join Devo 2.0, a generational "Kidz Bop" update of the eighties new wave band Devo. "Yes, it's awfully wonderful when your kid, who you think is the most talented person in the world, receives outside validation. But would the Hollywood experience she was about to encounter twist her innocent soul into something unrecognizable, or would she be able to manage it? Would I be able to protect her from this rough, unforgiving world? Was I a bad parent for even considering it?"

In the end Kimberly decided to let Jackie record and tour, and Jackie has been able to handle the tour and her success with grace and aplomb. "The lightening of my 'fear load,'" her mom told me, "gave both of us great freedom to take risks and experience life to its fullest."

We have a choice when we face difficult decisions: We can act with faith or we can act with fear. There are no guarantees except this one: If we dwell on our fears, we will definitely miss the joys of the unexpected.

Huffington Post commenter Lori Lenzer writes, "My resolve as a parent is to acknowledge guilt and fear and the other negative emotions that can haunt you as you contemplate your beloved child's complex and uncertain future . . . but not to let these feelings overwhelm me and take away the joy. If you do not do a good enough job guilt-tripping yourself, there are plenty of jerks out there who will do it for you. Try to laugh it off, go home, and give your children big hugs (if they still allow you to do this!) and embrace the day as well. Our time here is limited. Make the most of it."

IT TAKES A TRIBE

As we work through the endless challenges of parenting, there is no substitute for building a little tribe of family and friends around us. When I was growing up, raising children was always the task of an extended family that reached far beyond blood ties.

From the time I became a mother in 1989 until my own mother's death in 2000, she was devotedly involved in the raising of my daughters. And my sister has been like a second mother to them. Unfortunately, the extended family is now increasingly considered an Old World curiosity, like horse-drawn wagons and dinner conversation. Every time the child care crisis comes up for discussion, I wonder where are the grandmothers, where are the great-aunts, where are the grandfathers and the great-uncles? Languishing in senior citizens' homes? Watching soap operas? Playing bingo? Or spread across several time zones, waiting for their quarterly phone call and their yearly Hallmark card?

When, as a child, I ventured onto the streets of my neighborhood in Athens, I was never far from home because I had learned from my earliest experiences that every home was open to me and any woman on the block would mother me as surely as she would her own child — with a bandage, a spinach pie, a scolding, or a hug. It's hard to re-create that experience in America today, but we need to conjure up its spirit.

I learn a lot from talking with other mothers. It gives me perspective and the strength we get only when we're not alone. This has become all the more important to me since my mother's death, because being in her orbit made it much harder to cling to my fears. One of my last memories of her is at the kitchen table late at night, after she had made sure that everything had been taken care of around the house, writing longhand on a yellow pad her responses to an "Ask Yaya" section I had started on AriannaOnline, a Web site I had at the time. She had gone from standing up to the Nazis to dispensing online advice — mostly about fearless living — to people all over the world. And now the online community we have created on the Huffington Post is a place where parents can put politics aside and share their experiences. As Huffington Post commenter MJ Reynolds writes, "Talking with other parents and sharing our stories always helps me. I find that I am more understanding of the 'mistakes' made by friends or relatives than of my own. Being able to sit with friends and commiserate and laugh over our child's picky eating or refusal to wear shirts unless the neck tag is cut completely off helps me realize that we are more alike than different."

ABOVE ALL, LOVE UNCONDITIONALLY

The challenges I face raising my daughters are very different from the ones my mother confronted raising me. The world is a much more dangerous place. But some big truths haven't changed. We can't mother alone, we won't make the right decisions all the time, and there is no greater gift we can give our children than our unconditional love.

Children learn early enough that the world "out there" certainly does not love them unconditionally. Most of us make this discovery the first day we're sent into it alone, lunch boxes in our hands and fear in our hearts. So that early unconditional loving — which is not withdrawn when we fail to meet some standard of perfection — is a safe haven from which we can draw strength for the rest of our lives. I know I certainly have.

$\mathcal{K}$athy Eldon *on fearlessness*

ON JULY 12, 1993, my son, Dan Eldon, a Reuters photographer, was stoned to death by an angry mob in Mogadishu, Somalia. Dan and three colleagues had been summoned to the site of a brutal US bombing that had left scores of people dead and dying. Enraged survivors turned on the journalists. Dan was twenty-two.

In the weeks that followed I found it impossible to sleep or eat, haunted by images of Dan running from the mob. I feared I would never be at peace again, and I couldn't stop crying, overwhelmed by intense pain and anger — with the Somalis, with God, and most of all with myself.

After all, I had encouraged Dan to be a photographer. But also, I had encouraged him and his sister, Amy, to follow the message of the Oracle at Delphi to "know thyself," to seek their own truth and follow it — no matter what.

I'd heeded the words of the Oracle myself when I realized that I had to leave my husband. Dan supported my decision and did not make me feel guilty. Only after his death, when I read his journal, filled with the intense anxieties of an eighteen-year-old grappling with the disintegration of his family, did I understand his devastation.

In July 1992, home from UCLA, Dan heard rumors of a famine in Somalia and, with a young journalist, headed there, where he photographed haunting images that found their way into newspapers around the world. He went back again and again, postponing college. The experience changed him. I didn't know how to deal with the now troubled young man. For a few months, our communication was patchy and difficult.

Dan finally called me on my birthday, June 26, 1993. As we talked, he slowly began to open up about how worried he was that the horrific photographs he was taking might affect his mind. "Don't you think you've been there long enough?" I asked. "Isn't it time you came home?"

"I have to stay, Mom," he said. "My job isn't finished."

Suddenly I recalled how Dan had supported me on the most difficult decision I had ever made. "Okay," I answered. "No matter what, I'm proud of you."

"I love you," Dan said. "But we really need to talk. I'll send you a ticket to Nairobi."

The ticket never came. Two weeks later Dan was dead.

Amy and I later traveled to Somalia to film a TBS documentary, *Dying to Tell the Story,* profiling frontline journalists including Dan. But I still couldn't let go of my anger. It seemed nothing could release me from the pain.

Five months later, Amy and I were in New York for our film's premiere. In the cab on the way, I realized that our cabbie was Somali, and I told him about Dan. Ebrahim, the driver, listened carefully and said that his family, too, had suffered losses in the fighting. "I know all about your son and the journalists who died with him," he said gravely. "On behalf of all Somalis, I ask your forgiveness."

I realized the truth of Gandhi's message: "We must be the change we wish to see in the world." My healing came through sharing the stories of extraordinary people trying to make the world better. I now believe that Dan and I did what we had to do — I by teaching him the message of Delphi, and he by following his heart, no matter what.

Kathy Eldon is a documentary producer and author.

Fearless at Work

—◦—◦—

Free to Succeed

WORK HAS BEEN a central part of my life, just as it is for almost all women, including the 58 percent who are currently in the US labor force. Today, more than 70 percent of mothers work outside the home. I may never have worked in an office or been part of a corporate structure, but when I started looking at all the fears women face at work, I discovered that they were no different from the fundamental issues I've faced on my own career path. This was a lightbulb moment for me: Our work-related fears have little to do with whether we work in a forty-five-story office building or in our own homes. But they're intense and they're real, and I've seen them mirrored in the working lives of hundreds of women.

For most of us, work is a fundamental part of how we express ourselves in the world. It provides both identity and purpose. And thanks to the activism of generations of women (and men) in the last century, women have broken through into many traditionally male fields.

Our presence in powerful positions, on corporate boards, and as heads of our own businesses continues to grow. *Fortune* magazine reports that as of 2005, roughly half of all management and professional jobs were filled by women. In the last ten years, the number of Fortune 500 companies with at least one quarter of their boards filled with women directors went from eleven to sixty-four. And women now own 48 percent of small businesses.

That's all going in the right direction, but women are still not even close to parity, especially in pay. The compensation-package-half-empty view looks like this: According to Catalyst, a non-profit research group, women still account for just under 15 percent of Fortune 500 board members. And for the past ten years, the rate has been increasing only 0.5 percent a year. This means we won't hit the 50 percent mark until 2076 — a nice tricentennial present for America, but still, should it take three hundred years?

The slow pace of progress is not only bad for women, it's bad for the country. Numerous studies — not to mention centuries of real-world experience — tell us that women possess the smarts and skills to succeed in any job. But here's the catch (and one reason it's taken so long for women to break through): There is a professional double standard so that the same behaviors that help men get ahead and prove their worth on the job are discouraged in women. This double standard creates enormous fears in women: We are afraid of being too assertive, we are afraid of not being good enough, and we live with an all-purpose anxiety that has led many of us into lives of workaholism.

We have these fears for good reasons, as illustrated by the results of a famous psychological-assessment tool developed in the 1970s called the Bem Sex Role Inventory, or BSRI. It's based on a Stanford University project in which subjects were asked to list desirable adjectives for men and women. The male traits were all about being assertive, dominant, independent, and decisive. Those are all traits both genders should prize. But the desirable traits listed for women were all about relationships: loyal, compassionate, warm, cheerful, soft-spoken.

It's not just that toughness and decisiveness in women are often frowned upon and considered the exclusive province of men. It's also that the unique traits women bring to the workplace are being overlooked or dismissed as not valuable in a business context.

Institutionalized sexism and tradition are only part of the story, though. The other part is the role our own fears play, and how they hold us back from either attaining professional success or enjoying our achievements.

FEAR OF BEING AMBITIOUS AND ASSERTIVE

Aside from the office and career anxieties everyone faces, women have specific work-related fears that center on the paradox of maintaining relationships and remaining "feminine" while still doing a good job. These are the fears of ambition and assertiveness.

According to psychiatrist Anna Fels at Weill Medical College of Cornell University, "At each historical juncture where women have achieved access to social influence and recognition — legal and political rights, educational opportunities, career options — their capacity to be 'real women' has been impugned." Fels also notes the barrage of fear-mongering magazine articles and news stories that imply women have to choose between being a professional and being a good wife and/or mother.

The internalization of this fear begins at an early age. As Mary Pipher shows in *Reviving Ophelia,* girls begin life with just as much ambition as boys, but they slowly lose steam in adolescence, right when self-consciousness about gender roles begins to seep in.

The result is that women get the message loud and clear that ambition isn't feminine. Even when women are able to continue dreaming big, there's still a difference between the way our successes and those of men are received. When women succeed, we are much more likely than men to be uncomfortable with public acknowledgment of our success. We shuck off accolades — and any advancement that comes with them.

Indeed, when Fels began researching the role of ambition in women's lives, she found that the women she interviewed hated the very word *ambition:* "For them 'ambition' necessarily implied egotism, selfishness, self-aggrandizement, or the manipulative use of others for one's own ends. None of them would admit to being ambitious. Instead, the constant refrain was 'It's not me; it's the work.' . . . Clearly, these accomplished women were caught up in some sort of fear."

According to Fels, "The underlying problem has to do with cultural ideals of femininity. Women face the reality that to appear feminine, they must provide or relinquish scarce resources to others — and recognition is a scarce resource. Although women have more opportunities than ever before, they still come under social scrutiny that makes hard choices — such as when and whether to start a family or advance in the workplace — even harder."

The concept of femininity also interferes with a woman's ability to be assertive and aggressive. We so want to be liked that we worry about alienating people, so we often try to get what we want behind the scenes while still being careful to avoid seeming manipulative and disingenuous. It's nice to be nice, but it can be extremely draining and self-destructive when it mutes our voice, holds us back, and undermines our authenticity.

Fear of sticking our necks out because of how we'll be perceived often causes us to sabotage our careers. And the consequences of stifling ourselves aren't just financial. For example, Gail Evans, who worked her way from talk show booker to executive vice president of CNN, making her at the time the highest-ranking woman in broadcast journalism, says that even after she made it to the top of her field, she was still afraid to speak up at meetings. Instead, she'd let other people get credit for her ideas. "You'd think, as much power as I have there," she said in 2000, "that I could be comfortable saying anything . . . but I still hold back, I'm constantly censoring myself. And it's always a man who beats you to the punch."

In a MediaBistro seminar, Karen Salmansohn, author of *How to Succeed in Business Without a Penis,* observed that "men are more often warriors and women, worriers." Women, Salmansohn said, "want to be liked. This is something that starts very early on in life. They've done studies with little girls and little boys, and having lots of little girlfriends around us is very important to us. It doesn't go away when we get to be big girls, either. Guys know that in business nice guys finish last; girls don't know if nice girls finish last or if pushy, aggressive girls finish last."

We should, though. All we have to do is look at the science. A study in the *Journal of Occupational and Organizational Psychology* found that "agreeable people tend to self-sacrifice and compromise their own interests in order to make other people happy." If you're still not convinced, ask Lois P. Frankel, president of Corporate Coaching International and author of the book *Nice Girls Don't Get the Corner Office: 101 Unconscious Mistakes Women Make That Sabotage Their Careers.* She warns against acting "like a nice little girl" instead of an adult woman, and advises against acting obedient, asking permission, and being the last to speak — all nice and polite traits but likely to get you branded as a lightweight.

So the choice that many women see in the workplace is (a) be nice and demure, and just hope that someone notices and gives you a promotion, or (b) be assertive, get labeled pushy and aggressive, and hope you advance before becoming too hated. As most women know, it doesn't take too much to get labeled pushy and aggressive.

Who is responsible for this double standard — men or women? However it began, the answer right now is both. Deeply ingrained cultural ideals of femininity make it much harder for women to own up fearlessly to their ambitions and pursue them without apology. We pay the price in opportunity, achievement, success, and satisfaction.

FEAR OF FAILURE AND SUCCESS

Side by side with our fears of ambition and assertiveness we find our fear of failure. Sure, nobody likes to fail, but in many women the fear of failure translates into taking fewer risks and not reaching for our dreams. And the fear of not living up to some mythical ideal of perfection often means that many of us won't move ahead with a project or idea until we are 110 percent sure it's perfect, error-free, and unassailable. Which often means never moving ahead, or not moving as far or as fast as we could.

"Whenever I get a new job," Willow Bay, who has been a news anchor for CNN, ABC, and MSNBC, told me, "I am afraid that I won't be able to do it. It is practically a knee-jerk reaction. For a while I thought that was how everyone felt when they were faced with a new professional challenge. My husband, however, dispelled that comforting notion. He's never afraid in that way. He eagerly embraces new professional challenges without ever questioning his ability to deliver. He dives right in, while I'm much more of a dip-your-toe-in-the-water-first kind of girl."

According to a 2004 study by the Global Entrepreneurship Monitor, "Across all countries, a strong positive and significant correlation exists between a woman's belief of having the knowledge, skills, and experience required to start a new business and her likelihood of starting one. Conversely, a strong negative and significant correlation exists between fear of failure and a woman's likelihood of starting a new business."

Along with the fear of failure often comes the fear of success — the idea that if we go too far we will lose our connection to family and friends, to what's "real," and that men will be intimidated by us, making it even harder to sustain a relationship. This fear is related to our fear of assertiveness. But while this fear affects our *behavior* at work, fear of success undermines our very *dreams* of achievement.

Research by psychologist Matina Horner, former president of Radcliffe College, has demonstrated how fear of success affects women. She designed a personality test in which men and women were asked to write stories about a female and a male medical student. Nearly two-thirds of women's stories about the female med student showed a fear of rejection and concern about violating cultural standards of femininity. "If men and women can recognize autonomy and separate achievement," Horner said, "then the problem of fear of success might get solved." Especially when it comes to women's ambivalence about the prospect of earning more than their husbands. Karen Salmansohn calls this tendency the "keeping down with the Joneses syndrome."

A survey of Ivy League colleges confirmed women's concerns about standing out intellectually and how this would affect the way men saw them. Views that one might suppose had vanished at some point during the second term of Dwight Eisenhower are still alive and well — and flourishing in some of our top universities. No wonder we occupy so few directors' seats on the major corporate boards in this country.

Even successful professional women are not immune from these fears. "A friend of mine," Maureen Dowd wrote in her book *Are Men Necessary? When Sexes Collide,* "called nearly in tears the day she won a Pulitzer: 'Now,' she moaned, 'I'll never get a date!'"

DISCOURAGEMENT AND FEAR OF REJECTION

Another fear I've found that I share with most working women is born from a tendency to take criticism personally. In my work this fear manifested itself in getting editorial feedback. When I started writing in my twenties, it was as if every red mark and changed word was a personal rejection. Editorial sessions became battlegrounds: "I bandage your wounds and you keep cutting your veins," Fred Hills, my editor on *Maria Callas*, told me.

The most terrifying editing experience I've had was when my twice-a-week column began to be syndicated in the *Los Angeles Times*. The editorial-page editor at the time was Bob Berger. When I walked into his office for the first time, he greeted me with his signature gruff voice: "You're not at all what I thought you'd be like."

"What did you think I would be like?" I asked.

"I thought you would be like Melina Mercouri in *Topkapi*."

Given that even on my best days I'm no Melina Mercouri, my relationship with my new editor got off to a rocky start. A man with no patience for small talk, he would always answer the phone with a simple declarative "Bob!" — a greeting I found hard to respond to, since I was never able to comfortably bark back, "Arianna!" I invariably ended up feeling that whatever question I had was completely trivial compared to whatever big issues he was grappling with at the time. It got to the point where I would deliberately call when I knew he would be at lunch so that I wouldn't have to deal with all the childlike fears he evoked in me. Nine times out of ten, however, even this would fail because Bob, being Bob, would seldom spend more than ten minutes at lunch.

One day, we found ourselves talking about our kids, and somewhere between his talking about his son Luke and my talking about my daughter Isabella, I connected with him on a completely different level and stopped taking his critical feedback and his tone so personally. Bob, I discovered, had a crusty exterior but a marshmallow filling — like a Mallomar. I even got to the point where I welcomed the fact that his feedback was given bluntly and with no sugarcoating: "Too many rubber duckies in the first paragraph," he might say. I would then go back and rewrite and simplify. Bob's guiding maxim was one I could never hear often enough: Get to the point.

My relationship with Bob helped me reframe the whole editing process, to no longer think of it as personal criticism but rather as what it really is: an opportunity for improvement. And now I simply love being edited! In fact, knowing that there will be someone to catch me when I go too far has helped me take more risks as a writer.

THE DANGERS OF WORKAHOLISM

Fear creates insecurity. And insecurity creates another costly byproduct: workaholism. When we are afraid of failing, when we feel we constantly have to prove ourselves, we give priority to our jobs over everything and everyone else. This depletes our health and our spirits and keeps us in a state of constant tension.

When workaholism sets in, we sacrifice the important on the altar of the urgent. Our lives lose their balance and we lose our center. The problem often stems from a massive — and wrongheaded — redefinition of the urgent. It's no longer a matter of worrying about how we will deal with a blazing fire; instead it's the constant fear that a fire might start.

Part of this fear comes from a very sane place. As women, we know intuitively and from experience that we still don't "belong" in the male clubs that thrive at work. We also know that we can't play the game the same way men do or we will pay another kind of price. So what is left to us? Our own hard work. It's the one thing for which we are regularly applauded and recognized (even if that makes us uncomfortable). Hard work helps us fit in and gain a measure of security. And because hard work does indeed work, we do more and more and more of it until we can't stop.

Workaholism robs us of many things. In order to put in the hours, we sacrifice time with our families, our friends, and ourselves. We lose perspective about what is truly important to us and what is ultimately of enduring value. That's what happened to Holly Morris before she launched into a new life that led her to produce the award-winning PBS series *Adventure Divas*.

"It's hard to know exactly when the rigor mortis of the soul began to set in," Holly told me. "Maybe it was when the piles of paper on my desk took over, obscuring my vision of both the room and a self-determined future, or maybe it was when I found myself in the office for the third major holiday in a calendar year."

As well as depriving us of a lot of life and adventure, workaholism also deprives us of sleep. In fact, almost a third of working adults report having missed work or made errors at work because of sleep deprivation. The cost to US businesses from accidents and decreased productivity due to sleep deprivation is estimated at $150 billion annually.

Work always benefits from fresh ideas and new angles, but imagination and originality are the first casualties of sleep deprivation. Those aspiring to leadership should read their history. Thomas Jefferson, Winston Churchill, and Ronald Reagan were all renowned nappers. Believing that napping makes one less productive is, according to Churchill, "a foolish notion held by people who have no imagination."

And Bill Clinton, who is perhaps more identified than anyone on the planet with tirelessness and the lack of need for sleep, went even further. "Every important mistake I've made in my life," he said, "I've made because I was too tired."

Fear of assertiveness, fear of failure, and workaholism all conspire with one another to create a vicious cycle. We don't have all the opportunities men have, we're nervous about what opportunities we do have, we fear failure so we create situations that make it inevitable, we fear success so we either don't take risks or sabotage ourselves, we internalize what we perceive the criticisms might be were we to actually succeed, and we end up stressed, cranky, and afraid. There has to be a better way!

ON BECOMING FEARLESS AT WORK

Fearlessness gives us perspective on the role of work in our lives and will help us finally shatter the glass ceiling. But we need to conquer the workplace as women, in our own unique way, not as carbon copies of men — briefcase-carrying, pinstripe-wearing career machines who just happen to have vaginas.

María Otero is the CEO of the nonprofit ACCION International, which helps fund businesses for women in the developing world. "Being a woman makes me a better manager," she said. "In some ways, being able to develop a management-leadership style that is based on forming a team is very much in line with the way I interact with my sisters or other women. We're all in it together."

When Patricia Russo, the CEO of Lucent Technologies, was profiled in the *Star-Ledger* on the day it was announced that Lucent was merging with French telecom giant Alcatel, the opening line of the article was: "Patricia Russo, the second oldest of seven children, learned early in life how to nurture others." Can you imagine a profile of Jack Welch or Warren Buffett or Herb Allen beginning with an emphasis on his nurturing qualities? Yet nurturing her team helped Russo become one of only seven female chief executives of Fortune 500 companies.

Maria Rodale, vice chairman of Rodale, the wellness magazine and book publisher, had to overcome many fears when she inherited the business from her father: "When I was twenty-eight, my father was killed in a car accident in Moscow. I worked really hard to prove to the company's management at the time — and to my family — that I was worthy of the responsibility my father had left me. But it was never enough. We needed to make bold changes to bring Rodale out of debt and regain the trust of our customers. But did I have the courage to make them? Especially since they included asking longtime employees to leave. A lot of people didn't think that I, as a woman, would have the nerve to make such radical changes. But I did — and brought in CEO Steve Murphy, who made the company profitable again."

When she finally put aside the womanly need to please and focused on the task at hand, Rodale reinvented herself and the company, which has since been recognized with awards it had never received before and has produced bestsellers like *The South Beach Diet*. "Making risky business decisions," she says, "is still not easy, but I get up on my horse and go. It's my job and I love it."

MAKE BOLDNESS WORK FOR YOU

One way to overcome the fears of being ambitious and assertive is by learning how to play the men's office "game" but tailoring it to our own style. As Gail Evans observes in her book *Play Like a Man, Win Like a Woman,* knowledge of the men's rule book equals power in the workplace. Taking credit for our work and accomplishments and fearlessly negotiating for compensation can be interpreted as ambitious and aggressive. But as Evans says, "You are who you say you are." If you act timid and unimportant, that's how you'll be perceived.

We have to let go of the idea that we must be sweet all the time if we're going to be "real women." If my mother had worried about being polite when the Nazis rounded her up in the Greek mountains, she and the Jewish girls she was hiding would have been killed. She did what her fearless self knew she had to do.

Or, as Marin Alsop, the music director for the Baltimore Symphony Orchestra, says, "I'm passionate about people doing the best and being the best they can be, and sometimes you have to push people to do that. If everybody just loves you, you're probably not doing a very good job."

This doesn't mean we have to become obnoxious ogres. We can be assertive without sacrificing charm and humor. Humor especially can be very effective in taking the edge off being assertive. We can be a lot more challenging if we don't take ourselves too seriously. "Angels fly because they take themselves lightly," my mother used to remind us.

I learned the power of humor firsthand when I did "Strange Bedfellows" with Al Franken as part of Comedy Central's *Politically Incorrect* in 1996, at the Democratic National Convention in Chicago, the Republican National Convention in San Diego, and on election night in New York. Al and I sparred about politics from a specially constructed bed in the middle of the audience. It was, incidentally, the first and last time in my life I could actually get a tax deduction for lingerie. Suddenly people — especially young people — who ordinarily wouldn't waste a moment on politics became engaged, just by seeing political dialogue packaged in a different way, with humor and satire. It was a lesson that I took to heart and have regularly applied in speeches, TV appearances, and everyday working interactions.

Connecting with people on a personal level is also key. Even with those we interact with only at work, it's important to remember that their lives — their joys and their troubles — consist of much more than work. And the more at ease we are with ourselves — with our own emotions — the more able we'll be to reach out to others in a personal way.

It all comes down to what the French call *"être bien dans sa peau"* — to feel good in your own skin. It turns out it's as important at work as it is in the bedroom.

Adena Berkman Conway, founder of Berkman Fives, a New York career-development firm that caters to women, puts it this way: "If you work with all men, you might feel as though you have to be more assertive in order to be effective, but it might not feel like who you are. . . . Generally our advice is to incorporate pieces of yourself that do feel like yourself; find safe ways to show that these work, too, while at the same time maintaining the skills that are effective in getting you what you need."

Not surprisingly, the queen of "be who you are" agrees. "There is no moving up and out into the world," the world's first black female billionaire, Oprah Winfrey, says, "unless you are fully acquainted with who you are. You cannot move freely, speak freely, act freely, be free, unless you are comfortable with yourself."

GET PERSPECTIVE

Having perspective on what is important in our lives is another essential part of tapping into the boldness that allows us to fulfill our dreams. After two decades running a graphic design firm, Denise Houseberg stuck her neck out to start an Internet marketing business called MarketExpo.com, only to discover six months into it that she had breast cancer. "There was never a more important moment to have a project in which to pour all my angst," she says. "Breast cancer was the catalyst that removed a lifetime of fear. . . . Once you stare down the throat of your own demise and survive, you get pretty fearless about business matters. . . . I marched up to huge banks and said, 'Hey, I need a $125,000 line of credit, and I don't want to pay a lot for it right now.' Most banks scoffed at me, but when I got to JPMorgan Chase, a rep there said, 'We'll send someone over with the papers for you to sign.' Before my illness, I would have been like most women, who say, 'What does it hurt to bootstrap, use my own money, and build things slowly?'"

Facing a life-threatening illness is an unfortunate way to learn the lesson that it doesn't hurt to be bold and assertive. Another way is to jump into a big new public venture. A few years ago, environmental activist Laurie David and I — together with film producer Lawrence Bender, writer-director Scott Burns, and talent agent Ari Emanuel — launched the Detroit Project and a series of commercials designed to get people to connect the dots between our addiction to gas-guzzling SUVs and foreign-produced oil, and how that money was being used to fund terrorism. "The scariest experience for me," Laurie remembers, "was getting into bed one night after our campaign was launched and accidentally turning the radio to a right-wing station and hearing the talk show host going to town, screaming, 'Who is this Laurie David? Who does she think she is, telling us what to drive?' He was just ripping into us with horrendous personal attacks. I remember shaking, just shaking."

The next morning, Laurie and I went on a hike. She was really upset and really afraid. A week later, she got a call from Bobby Kennedy, the passionate environmental activist. He told her the ads had knocked his socks off. "You know, Laurie," he said, "you can't change the world and not have people come after you who don't *want* you to change the world."

"That was the moment for me," she says, "when I realized that if I was going to have an impact on these issues I deeply cared about, I was going to have to accept criticism and not let it paralyze me."

OVERCOMING FEAR OF FAILURE

Not letting our fears paralyze us is key in any new job or venture, especially when there is the possibility of public criticism or humiliation. We have to weigh the psychic cost of not trying against the possibility of not succeeding and being embarrassed by our efforts. The former creates regret, the latter a few hours — or maybe a few days — of licking our wounds.

If you want to succeed big, there is no substitute for simply sticking your neck out. That's how Mellody Hobson, president of

Ariel Capital Management, a multibillion-dollar asset management firm based in Chicago, helped build the company. She told me how she succeeded in landing a huge client: "I was pitching the head of pensions at United Airlines. 'Why would I hire you?' he asked. 'If I could,' I replied, 'I'd jump on the table, grab you by the lapels, and tell you, "This is the best decision you will ever make."' We got the account. He joked that no one had ever put it like that."

One woman who became a symbol of fearlessness at work in the nineties was Murphy Brown. Okay, she's fictional, but there was a reason the show touched a nerve. She was a single woman devoted to her career who said what she meant and meant what she said.

Not surprisingly, Diane English, the woman who created the character, and Candice Bergen, the woman who so brilliantly brought the character to life, are both prime examples of overcoming fears. When Diane English first proposed Candice Bergen for the role, CBS and Warner Brothers categorically said no. Bergen was deemed "too elegant." But English was absolutely convinced that it had to be Bergen, and her conviction made her fearless. She walked into the CBS president's office and, as she put it, "closed the door and actually refused to leave until he said yes."

"Diane shoved me down their throats," Candice Bergen remembers. "Then I panicked because, while I had the instinct that I would be able to pull it off, I hadn't worked in so long, since I'd had my daughter. I really wasn't sure if I'd be able to do it, and I was very, very frightened." But she didn't let her fears stop her and, as the world knows, went on to become a cultural icon and win five Emmys.

Detective Olivia Benson in *Law and Order: Special Victims Unit* is another fearless role model for women — including teenagers like my daughter Christina.

"When I got the part," Mariska Hargitay told me, "I was given this gift of playing someone who was so different from who I was. Olivia's fearlessness defines her. She looks at a situation, feels the fear, then does what she has to do anyway. Young women really respond to that. They feel their own strength in her. Women are always saying to me, 'Oh, I wish I could be like Olivia,' and I say, 'You are, because if you didn't have that same strength inside you, you wouldn't recognize it in her, you wouldn't identify with her.'

"The character has been such a teacher to me. When I am playing a scene, and I am standing there with my gun drawn, with someone's life on the line, I have this incredible experience of the importance of the goal overtaking the fear. So I've been trying to apply that principle to my *own* life, whether the goal is a relationship or public speaking or pushing through a personal boundary — or becoming a mother! Instead of focusing on my fear, I focus on the goal, the prize waiting at the end of the race. I think life pays off really big if you live it like that."

And when there's a big new challenge to face, we can always improvise ways to master our fears. Willow Bay, for example, deconstructs new assignments into manageable chunks. "The step-by-step process of preparation acts as a broom sweeping away the dust of fear and clearing the path for success."

At any point, of course, we can get discouraged, feel rejected, and doubt ourselves. At such times, we just need to keep plugging on — and often, in surprising ways, hurdles become stepping-stones and our fears are dispersed.

THE ART OF NEGOTIATION

Some of us try to get what we want through workaholism, but there's another way: negotiation. The art of asking for what you want is a key to fearlessness at work.

All successful negotiation begins with being crystal clear about what you want. Many women shrink from the idea of negotiating because they think it just means being loud, aggressive, and pushy. In fact, the essence of negotiation is coming to an agreement that does not sacrifice what is essential to you while allowing the other party to do the same. It's actually something women are brilliantly suited for.

Vera Rubin is an astronomer who has made important discoveries about the phenomenon of dark matter and how galaxies move. She managed to negotiate for herself a high-powered science career at the Carnegie Institution of Washington *and* time at home with her kids: "I wanted to go home at 3:00 p.m. every day," she says, "so they offered two-thirds of the salary I was getting. . . . There had never been a woman staff member. Ten years later, I asked to be paid full-time, and I was. Then I said, 'I'm still going home at three.'"

Vera could negotiate because she felt secure in her value to the institute. But many women don't feel safe negotiating — it makes us feel insecure. Watch a man negotiate — and Carnegie Mellon University research shows that men are four times more comfortable negotiating a first salary than women — and there's a quality of gamesmanship involved. Indeed, the men in the study compared negotiating to "winning a ball game," whereas the women said the process felt like "going to the dentist." But what's the worst that can happen? We are told no, and we're no worse off than we were before. Just look around and you'll see plenty of evidence that asking for what we want results not in the realization of our worst fears but in getting what we want.

Romi Lassally, the features editor of the Huffington Post, learned this when she was president of a film production company and, according to her contract, was entitled to a bonus for one of her movies. "Even though I had the terms of my deal in writing," she told me, "I was a nervous wreck as I sat in my boss's office and asked for the bonus. 'Do you really think you deserve to be paid a bonus for this movie?' he asked. 'You make a very nice salary. . . . Shouldn't that cover all the work you do here?'

"I was stunned by his remark. But I was also shocked by my reaction to it. Sure, he had stirred a healthy dose of indignation in me, but he had also tapped into my deepest insecurities that I wasn't worthy, that, contract or no contract, perhaps I *didn't* deserve to be paid extra. I felt like a frightened little girl and was overwhelmed by the feeling that I'd overstepped my bounds. I never saw that bonus, but my story has a happy ending. When it came time for me to leave that company, we made an agreement that I would receive bonuses if two of my movies were ever made. The movies did get made, and although it took many years and many legal letters, I was eventually paid on both of them."

MAKE FEAR YOUR FRIEND

As in other areas of life, being fearless at work doesn't mean eliminating fear. It simply means acknowledging it, making it your ally, and not letting it stop you.

Actress Christine Lahti, who is also a director (in a very male-dominated field), told me: "Almost every time I take on a new role (or a new directing job), I have some fear. Even though fear can sometimes make me want to vomit, I crave that fear; it means I am challenging myself, and I feel it can be a positive, exciting energy. I teach my children to always try to go toward that which they fear (except when it's physically dangerous). In a play or a film, I use my fear or nervousness in almost every scene I'm in. Because usually every scene involves some high stakes, the character is often nervous or fearful. I actually depend on fear in my work to help me keep the stakes high in the scene. I think fear is a natural thing and can actually enhance one's life rather than diminish it if one can recognize it, accept it, and use it. It can be very exciting to challenge yourself in that way."

It's been very important for me to learn to recognize when, especially at work, I am affected by other people's fears. Because fear is not only common in competitive workplaces, it's also contagious. In a study of diversity, conflict, and performance in the workplace, Brian Kulik of Washington State University found that "expressions of fear lead to fearful affect in groups; conversely, expressions of fearlessness may lead to fearlessness among individuals in groups." So the good news is that confidence is also contagious, and people who express fearlessness engender confidence in others.

One thing that can help on the journey to fearlessness is trusting that even when our worst fears are realized, things can still wind up working out our way. That's what happened to Willow Bay. As a former television anchor, she is well versed in delivering the news. But, she admits, give her a spot quiz — even an at-home game of Jeopardy — and she panics. "If I have to answer questions involving names, dates, or historical references, I'm seized with fear and I freeze," she explains. "After a two-year hiatus, I was offered a job at MSNBC. I was itching to get back on the air, but then they told me about their 'screen test.'

"The purpose was to see how I would handle breaking news. I was asked to read the teleprompter, and then, in my earpiece, I hear, 'The pope had a heart attack.' I froze midsentence. Being put on the spot like that was way too much like Jeopardy for me. I forgot the pope's name. I forgot his age, his last hospital stay for pneumonia just the month before. I panicked. Then moments later there was another voice in my ear: 'Helicopter down in Fallujah.' That one I handled a bit better, but the victory was short-lived. Next comes 'Reports of a corpse believed to be Jimmy Hoffa surfacing in Secaucus.' Oh God, remind me again when Jimmy Hoffa went missing? He was a mob boss, right? Get me out of here now! I want to go home. I knew it was a disaster.

"The next day I got a call from the head of the network. 'Well, you failed your screen test,' he said. I could feel the pounding in my ears. 'But when you're in the studio again, it will come back like riding a bike.'

"I was incredibly relieved — but now even more anxious about getting back in the anchor chair. So I hired a media coach and spent an afternoon dusting off the cobwebs. And that made all the difference. It was an important reminder of what I *could* do instead of what I couldn't. When I did go back on the air, my timing was a little off, but, just as my boss had predicted, it was like riding a bike."

Again and again, we find that our resources allow us to bounce back professionally. In 2002, Caroline Graham, the former West Coast editor of *Vanity Fair, The New Yorker,* and *Talk* magazine, and her good friend editor in chief Tina Brown both lost their jobs after Harvey Weinstein, *Talk's* publisher, decided to close the magazine.

At first, Caroline felt "shame and fear. I had no nest egg, four children, a house, and several dogs to take care of." But she rallied and applied her professional skills — and the relationships she'd nurtured — to a new career running C4 Consulting, a marketing, public-relations, and event-planning firm: "In that emergency I got on the phone to those who had trusted me in the past and those who might need the expertise I had gained. I learned that I had more friends and more knowledge than I had imagined. My son Charlie pitched in as my partner, and we went at it like terriers. And it worked. Fighting fear was invigorating, and so was taking on the world in my way."

THE REWARDS OF BEING FEARLESS AT WORK

Ultimately, to be fearless at work means to find a sense of self-determination, accomplishment, fulfillment, and purpose that helps us live our best lives.

What's more, by being a leader at work — taking risks and doing things in new ways — we can mentor and show others the way to not only excel but transform the meaning of work. That's what Anna Quindlen urged during her speech to the Women's Commission for Refugee Women and Children: "Was the point of this great social revolution to have corner offices, fat retainers, and retirement accounts? Did we want the right to lead imitation men's lives? Or did we really want something that we haven't quite gotten yet, the ability to put our grand stamp on the ethos of the entire world? . . . We're at a moment of synthesis, of balance, a middle ground. And that is the point at which we realize that work, influence, even power with no countervailing forces, no intimacy, no family, no sense of connection to others, is for many of us no kind of life at all."

Pattie Sellers, editor at large of *Fortune,* who has talked to hundreds of top women professionals for the magazine's annual "Most Powerful Women in Business" list, described to me how she has experienced powerful women reframing the purpose and meaning of work: "Men tend to look at power vertically — it's all about reaching the bigger job, the next rung on the ladder. This is somewhat of a stereotype, but research and all my interviews with powerful women and powerful men over the past decade suggest that men are much less distracted from that vertical view than women, who view success more horizontally, with a much wider peripheral vision.

"To women leaders like Avon CEO Andrea Jung and Oprah Winfrey, power is about a broad landscape of influence. (Jung told me that she defines power as 'the privilege to influence.' Oprah says that power is 'the ability to impact with purpose.') These women are generally not satisfied by simply climbing the ladder to the bigger job and the bigger title."

As journalist Patt Morrison likes to say, "The entire point of having power is to use it on behalf of people who don't have it."

This is how Mellody Hobson puts it: "I haven't even scratched the surface in terms of what I want to be, what I want to achieve, what I want to contribute, and what effect I want to have in society. What trees do I plant, what do I leave behind?"

One element that fearless women share is the sense that there is always more — more challenges to face, more risks to take, more failures to overcome, more influence to have, more successes to revel in, more trees to plant.

Melina Kanakaredes on fearlessness

As THE YOUNGEST of three girls born into a traditional yet strangely modern Greek American family, I was taught to be fearless about most everything. However, *fearless* would never have been defined as life with no fear. In fact, it was quite the opposite. I was your average kid who had enough healthy fear to get good grades, stay away from drugs, and keep boys at a distance . . . sort of. As I grew up, I realized that the outcome of all these fears was positive. In fact, every time I was fearful about something, somehow that fear enabled me to grow.

This enlightened me to the fact that I both needed and wanted to scare myself. After all, in my mind, if I wasn't a little frightened of something, I was just coasting through life. With the right approach to fear, obstacles can become opportunities and dreams can become realities.

Fearing that I'd never be the person my grandparents sacrificed for, I went to college and received both a BFA in musical theater and a minor in psychology. Fearing the idea that I would never get the opportunity to act on stage professionally, I moved to New York after college. Fearing that I'd get used to the quick cash, I allowed myself to work only three days a week at my "day job." I purposely stayed hungry to force myself to make a living at my craft. I could give at least a hundred other personal examples. However, I shall spare you the details and say only this: *Just do it! Get scared!* Shake things up a bit. You can't win the lottery without buying the ticket.

I live by this philosophy every day, both in my personal life and my career. It's fear that inspired me to start directing, producing, and, most recently, to parlay my acting into writing. I'd never written before, and I was scared out of my mind. In the end, I sold my first pilot script. Who'da thunk it? I say embrace your fears, meet them head-on. My guess is they were given to us for a reason.

Melina Kanakaredes is currently starring in CSI: NY.

$\mathcal{F}$earless About Money

The Key to Abundance

WOMEN, MONEY, AND work — talk about a triangulated relationship. Money is, of course, inextricably tied up with work. It's what we get in return for our labor, it's how we pay our bills, it's what we devote an enormous share of our lives to making. And, yes, that's true for both men and women. But for women there's an added twist: How do we earn what we're worth in a world that still pays us seventy-eight cents to a man's earned dollar? The answer: fearlessness.

But it's hard to be fearless about something that is so elemental — so wrapped up with survival. And even if we have an adequate income, "poverty consciousness" — the fear that no matter how much we have, it's never enough — can fill us with gut-gripping terror. Some of the richest women I know are still driven by the fear of ending up as bag ladies.

Sometimes poverty consciousness becomes a motivator. Melody Hobson is a remarkable success story: At thirty-seven, she's one of the wealthiest and most influential African American women in the country. "I'll always be thankful for what I've been given," she told me. But a tumultuous, financially unstable home life as a child instilled in her the fear of being penniless, a fear that's been both a positive motivator and a source of constant anxiety.

"I had no sense of security," she says, "and was always worried about money even as a small child. So I resolved that I would never have to struggle. I even made a vow to myself: 'I am going to be rich! I can't live like that.'" Money for Mellody represented freedom — and choices. But even now she wonders, "What if I screw up and lose everything? What is the amount of money that would make me comfortable? And my number is always much higher than my friends'." When she could, she'd even pay her phone bill and mortgage for an entire year. "So if everything goes wrong, I'd at least have a phone and a place to live." Money fears can be so strong, and sometimes irrational, that even Mellody, with all her financial success, can't completely banish hers.

We pursue wealth with the hope that it can vanquish fear, but sometimes the relentless acquisition of money is simply a manifestation of other fears. "Money is very powerful," says Maria Young, a financial educator at Rutgers University, "and people have emotional needs that they try to satisfy with money."

WHAT MONEY REPRESENTS

So money isn't just money — it's also a stand-in for our fears. We fear we will never have the resources to live well, parent well, feel secure. For both genders, money symbolizes so much in our culture and our lives. We use it to measure our achievements; we use it as a barometer of our success. We may not like to think about class, but we still use money to determine all sorts of social hierarchies, whether in the boardroom or in the parking lot of our kids' school.

Of course compulsive comparisons as well as compulsive spending and compulsive hoarding can be symptoms of the same thing: an emptiness in other parts of our lives that we try to fill with what money can buy. When this is the case, no amount of spending or accumulating or climbing up some mythical hierarchy is going to solve the underlying problems. As Mellody Hobson puts it, women should do their best to handle their finances but remember that "angst won't be satiated by the size of your bank account."

Money fears are universal, but it's also true that women relate to money differently than men do. "Money represents love, power, security, control, self-worth, independence," says psychotherapist Olivia Mellan. "If money was just money, everyone would make rational decisions about it." We know women certainly don't always do that. But why? One reason is that women have been raised to think of money in terms of security — and not just financial security. Even today, a surprising number of us still think that it's the man's job to make and understand money. Far too often we delegate this responsibility and don't learn enough about money — so of course we fear it.

That's where we have to start. We can never be fearless about money until we demystify it and take charge of it.

TAKING HOLD OF THE PURSE STRINGS

The simple facts are these: Women make less money than men, we save less for retirement, and we usually outlive our husbands if we have them. Women represent the majority of the elderly poor. And, as Harvard's Elizabeth Warren and her daughter Amelia Warren Tyagi report in their book *The Two-Income Trap,* the number one indicator that a woman will go broke is the birth of a child.

Men are conditioned from a young age to go after what they want. Not only are they rewarded by actually getting what they ask for, they're also rewarded, in a larger sense, for even asking. Not so with women. We feel guilty when we ask for — or, God forbid, demand — what we feel we're entitled to. As Galia Gichon, a financial adviser who owns the company Down-to-Earth Finance, puts it, "We sort of let ourselves be told what we're worth instead of just stating very directly and confidently what we feel we deserve." Making demands is not considered ladylike.

The dynamic behind this behavior is not even strictly about money — it's just another manifestation of fear. "People I've worked with who have taken control of their money," Gichon has said, "have seen results in other parts of their life. Career, personal life — there's no question about it, they all work together."

I've been rich and I've been poor, so I've seen this in my own life. I know what money is and what it's not, what it can do and what it cannot. We need to put money into proper perspective in our lives, stop avoiding it, learn about it, and stop making it more important than it is.

FOR LOVE OR MONEY (COUPLING AND UNCOUPLING)
For Carol Hoenig, financial dependence was one of the things that kept her in an unhappy marriage. "Eighteen months after

we were married," she said, "we began our family and I was a stay-at-home mom. Over the years, when I wanted more from my marriage, there was the consistent threat that if I wasn't happy, I could move out. Because I didn't work outside the home, I had few options, and he took comfort in that. It's easy to keep someone under your control when you bring home the money."

Eventually, she decided to pursue her own interests and went back to school, which changed everything. "I always enjoyed writing but never dared believe that I could make a living at it, until I took a number of college courses and was given encouragement by my professors. I then got a part-time job working in a bookstore and was immediately promoted to full-time. While my children were growing up, I was, too. My writing and my career were empowering. Finally, I acknowledged the fact that my husband was not invested in the marriage and he never would be. I was also becoming stronger as a person and realized that I would be happier on my own."

I saw a similar dynamic in my mother's relationship with my father, although with her innate fearlessness, she did not let financial concerns stop her from leaving him when I was eleven years old. For my father, as for many Greek men of his generation, there was nothing wrong with extramarital affairs. "I don't want you to interfere with my private life," I remember him telling my mother when she complained. His marriage was part of his public life, his affairs part of his private life. But that was not okay for her, and even though she had no job and no obvious way to earn money, she took her two children and left, trusting that somehow she would make ends meet. And, somehow, she did.

To complicate matters even further, many men seem to be

uncomfortable with women who are financially independent, because with money comes power and confidence. And many men are still threatened by powerful, confident women. It breaks down roughly like this: Men love women. Men love money. But men don't love women with money. A bit reductive, but this has recently been confirmed by actual scientific data. A 2004 study found that, as the *New York Times* put it, men would rather marry "their secretaries than their bosses."

This is perplexing because men are supposed to be all about problem-solving and efficiency. If you love women and you love money, then wouldn't a rich woman be a twofer, like one of those phone–MP3 players? So why does money enhance the male ego in one instance but diminish it in another?

A quick answer might be that it's really more about age — that men prefer younger women, who happen to be more likely to have less money and fewer accomplishments and thus are less threatening to them. But that's certainly not always true. How, for instance, do you explain thirty-something actor Jude Law, who cheated on his beautiful, successful twenty-three-year-old fiancée with his children's twenty-six-year-old nanny?

You'd think that as women continue to make gains in the workplace it would be easier if men just learned not to be threatened by women with money. But that's probably not going to happen anytime soon. Money gives women independence and power, and many men still derive their sense of personal value from their ability to provide for and take care of women. When a woman's independence clashes with a man's self-image, it can disrupt a relationship. Until that changes, women who have become financially successful might want to take another lesson from the male-dominated corporate world and hide their assets from potential mates. Or hire only really, really wealthy nannies.

All joking aside, becoming fearless about money doesn't necessarily mean that we'll become wealthy, but it does mean that no matter what happens to us financially, or romantically, we'll have more say about it and more options. And having more confidence in life, and in our relationships, is always a good thing.

Entrepreneur Jody Miller summoned her courage to launch the Business Talent Group, a new marketplace for top independent professionals, in order to have greater control over her life. "I decided," she said, "to raise several million dollars from people I knew rather than institutional investment funds. People say they 'love' you and want to back you, but until you ask, you don't know. Any time you put 'love' to the test, you make yourself vulnerable. But unlike love, you can't take business rejection personally.

"When you raise money, you can't be afraid to ask for what you want. You need to remember that you're not asking for a favor — you're offering an opportunity."

Jody's strategy would not have worked if she hadn't overcome the fear of putting herself out there in the first place. She told me: "Two things helped me overcome the fear of jumping in: First, I looked at who else was raising money. I saw a lot of people with a lot less experience than I had — if they could do it, I could do it. Also, I had read that the founders of the highly successful Blackstone Group were rejected by hundreds of people before they got their funding. Second, I focused on the 'prize.' I knew nothing would be more rewarding than creating a company on my terms that changed things for talented people."

ON BECOMING FEARLESS ABOUT MONEY

I remember during the last presidential primaries watching together with my fourteen-year-old daughter Diane Sawyer's interview of Judy Dean. I found myself touched in a way I rarely have been during the countless hours I've spent watching this kind of political theater. "Why are you tearing up, Mom?" my daughter asked me near the end of the segment. I had to think about it. What about Mrs. Dean's decidedly unpolished responses had gotten to me? Then it hit me: the birthday rhododendron.

Judy Dean had actually been genuinely pleased when her husband had given her one of the perennial shrubs for her fiftieth birthday. "I'm not a very 'thing' person," she explained. "Everything I want, I have — I'm not that interested in things." And that was that. A simple, sincere summons to simplicity.

People like Judy Dean stand in stark contrast to our national obsession with consumption. Our "Supersize Me!" society has so elevated the manufactured over the meaningful that when somebody dares question the value of our collective covetousness, we react as though they've impugned the legitimacy of the sacred scrolls of the Scriptures. It's hardly surprising that self-storage space is now two billion square feet in America — more than three times the size of Manhattan. We keep buying stuff even though we have nowhere to put it.

The antithesis of all this was my mother. She was the ultimate non-thing person. When she died, she left behind no prized possessions — not surprising considering her habit of giving such things away. For instance, there was the time we tried to give her a second watch for her birthday, only to have her give it to someone else two days later. "I already have a watch," she explained.

She told me once that she operated like the government: she first decided what it was that her children needed and then she set out to find the money. My mother was one of the original deficit financers. She made ends meet by borrowing or by selling her possessions, from a carpet brought by her parents from Russia to her last pair of gold earrings. I'm not advocating credit card debt — far from it. The point is that my mother's real wealth was the fact that she never made decisions from a place of lack. Even when she and my sister and I had to share a one-bedroom apartment in Athens, she always radiated abundance. When I said I wanted to go to Cambridge, she never said, "We don't have the money." Which we didn't. She was a dreamer and always believed that the universe would conspire to bring forward the resources to fulfill her dreams. Which in her case were all dreams for her daughters.

GIVE AND YOU SHALL RECEIVE

When I started making money — after my biography of Maria Callas became a big bestseller — my mother saw this financial success only as a passport to freedom, which for her meant never having to make decisions based simply on the price tag. She taught my sister and me all about abundance: that it has more to do with your state of mind than your actual bank balance. And she was constantly living in a state of offering. Food, of course, was her favorite thing to offer, but it was a metaphor for so much more. I'm convinced that she absolutely believed that something terrible would happen to her children — and her grandchildren and her friends — if they went twenty minutes without eating. Nobody could ring our doorbell, whether the Federal Express man or a parent dropping off a child for a playdate, without being asked, indeed urged, to sit down and try whatever she was cooking in the kitchen. And nobody could leave our house without goody bags filled with food.

I may not greet the UPS driver with a plate of food, but I have learned that every time I give something away, it reinforces how abundant I feel my life is. Ten years ago, I began tithing 10 percent of my income to charity. Tithing is one of the oldest spiritual principles; it acknowledges that we are not alone in the universe and that when we give back without fear, we open ourselves to receiving more. Each donation makes me grateful that I'm able to give and makes me value the act of giving and recognizing in the moment — rather than in retrospect — the blessings in my life. "What a wonderful life I've had," the French author Colette said. "I only wish I had realized it sooner."

PURSUE YOUR PASSION

True fearlessness about money can come only when we are not driven by an insatiable desire for security but have begun living a life driven by passion and purpose, regardless of our specific financial circumstances.

I remember when I was in my midtwenties and writing my second book. My first book, *The Female Woman,* had been a surprise success. Instead of accepting any one of the book contracts I had been offered to write on women again, I decided to tackle a subject I'd been preoccupied with through college (and indeed remain preoccupied with today): the role of leaders in shaping our world. I locked myself in my London flat and worked around the clock on this book. I would write until I couldn't stay awake — sometimes into the early hours of the morning.

The book was finally finished, and I don't remember ever before or since having been as happy with the work I'd done. So imagine my surprise when publisher after publisher rejected it. Indeed, thirty-six publishers turned it down before Stein & Day finally published *After Reason* in the United States. It was the kind of rejection that brought up all kinds of self-doubt, including fears that I not only was on the wrong career path but was going to go broke in the process. "What if the success of my first book was a fluke, and I was not really meant to be a writer?" I would ask myself in the middle of many a sleepless night. And this was, after all, not just a theoretical question; it was also a crassly financial one. "How am I going to pay my bills?" I had used the royalties from my first book to subsidize writing the second, and now that money was running out. My choice was to get some kind of "real" job while pursuing my writing or get a loan.

My desire to write turned out to be stronger than my fear of poverty. Had I been afraid, I might have tossed the manuscript in the wastebasket somewhere around rejection letter fifteen and taken a job that had nothing to do with my passion. Instead, I walked into Barclays Bank in St. James Square in London and met with a banker named Ian Bell. With nothing more to offer than a lot of Greek chutzpah, I asked him for a loan. And with a lot of unfounded trust, he gave it to me.

I've always been grateful to Ian Bell. He was, after all, the person who made it possible for me to write a book that, although never a commercial success, garnered lots of good reviews. More important, the book was like a seed planted in my twenties that finally sprouted in my forties when I became seriously engaged in politics.

Abundant passion and abundant hope (not to mention abundant nerve!) pushed me past my financial fears. It is impossible to be fearless about money if we don't value other parts of our lives and ourselves more than we value our bank accounts.

Marcy Carsey on fearlessness

I HAVE A fearless mother. Any discussion about fear or my lack of it starts, and nearly ends, there.

My mother and father taught me the meaning and meaninglessness of money. His job at the shipyard never brought much, but they tithed at the church, and there was always something for anyone who needed it. Money meant only what it should mean: a roof over our heads, food on the table, and the means to help anyone with less. There was never a thought of envy, status, or worry associated with money. I know that the reason I was able to make money in business is because I could risk it. I didn't need it; I didn't love it. It was just a side effect of doing work I loved.

My mother taught me about work, too. She got a job at seventeen to support her mother and put her older sister through college. She was young, but she was feisty. When her boss scolded her one day for being a few minutes late, she showed him the time sheet and pointed out that she had worked overtime most nights that month. Without pay. She was proud of her work, and she would take no guff about shirking responsibilities. This was around the Depression, when people were lined up for any job, and employers knew it. Fearless. When as a teenager I was fired from my first job, behind the counter of a coffee shop, and was convinced that I would be a hard-core unemployable for the rest of my life, my mother wasted no time. She fired up the Dodge, told me to get in, and drove me the twenty miles into Boston to a temp agency. By that afternoon, I had a filing job. "Don't evah worry, honey. . . . There's always another job for a smaht girl like you. Just climb back on the hoss." (This was New England, after all.)

And somehow, without ever saying it outright, but by living it, my mother taught me that anything's possible. There are no limits to what a "smaht girl" can do. Pretty never counted, position never counted, but the adventure that was life did count. She taught me to jump in, with joy and moxie, and take it on.

My mother is ninety-eight now and lives with me. Her eyes still sparkle with good humor, and the moxie is intact. But she's winding down, surely and gracefully, like a beautiful old clock. And this brings me to what I do fear. Nothing scares me more than the people I love being lost to me or having to suffer. The only time I ever saw anything close to fear in my mother's eyes was when my brother was lost at sea. Or when our country doctor told her I would go deaf if he couldn't keep a throat infection under control. Or even when our cat came home in horrific shape after a fight. (For the record, my brother was found, I can hear a snarky remark from my daughter three rooms away, and the cat lived to a ripe old age.) You give over to those you love the key to your peace of mind and you never get it back.

So even my mother was not without fear. And none of us can ever claim to be so. But she taught me to put it in its place. And there it has stayed.

Marcy Carsey is cofounder of Carsey-Werner, producer of The Cosby Show *and* Roseanne, *among many other programs.*

$\mathcal{F}$earless About Aging and Illness

Time Can Be on Your Side

IN A CULTURE that values youth as much as ours does, from our standards of beauty to the fact that only one demographic — eighteen to thirty-four — seems to matter to advertisers, time is Public Enemy #1. Especially for women.

Every new wrinkle or gray hair can send fear shooting through us: the fear of losing the power of youth, the fear of being stigmatized as "over the hill."

Nowhere is this trend better illustrated than at our popular culture's temple, the movie theater. Back in the 1950s, studio executives regularly lied about their stars' ages, depending on what they thought would most appeal to the public. As Harlan Boll, a movie publicist, put it, "The American public doesn't really forgive people for getting older."

This is borne out in a study done by the Screen Actors Guild in 2000. After forty, male actors get 60 percent more work than female actors do, and as a result they tend to have longer careers than their female counterparts. In writing about this study, the

Girls, Women & Media Project has noted, "That's a difference of about 7,000 jobs and millions of dollars a year. . . . Quick: Name a female action hero, host of a TV show, or series lead over sixty years old."

Of course, unforgiving notions about aging are not limited to show business and the arts. In real life, too, older women are cast aside for younger "trophy wives" or younger trophy mistresses. We fear — and not without reason — that advancing age can leave us undesirable and alone.

It's no wonder that women do all they can to keep their age a secret. In fact, when Nancy Alspaugh and Marilyn Kentz wrote their book *Fearless Women: Midlife Portraits,* about women over fifty making the best of their lives, they had an incredibly hard time finding celebrities willing to admit their real age.

It's hard to be fearless in the world if you're afraid to let the world know how long you've been in it! I'd like to say I was always fearless about age, but in my case, I had no choice. When my first book came out, I was twenty-three, and my publisher — seizing on my youth as a marketing device — trumpeted my date of birth on the dust jacket. My age won't be a part of the marketing campaign for this book, but it's definitely not a secret. (To save some Googling, I was born on July 15, 1950, and, for those interested, Cancer sun, Cancer moon, and Scorpio rising.)

With aging, the fears aren't just about looks or our bodies not being able to do everything they once could. There is also the fear of being dependent, vulnerable, disregarded, and isolated. And it's a legitimate fear: In our culture, as Mary Pipher writes in *Another Country: Navigating the Emotional Terrain of Our Elders,* "We are xenophobic toward our old people."

For every Tina Turner or Diane Keaton who is celebrated, thriving, and in charge of her own life, there are thousands of older women who are cast aside and marginalized, their wisdom and experience a wasted resource. In fact, we've taken to segregating the elderly from the rest of society, shipping them off to nursing homes as if we are afraid they might contaminate us. Or simply remind us where we'll be in a few years or decades.

SICK ABOUT GETTING SICK

We can hide our fear of old age with out-of-sight, out-of-mind thinking, but we can't do the same with illness.

I was forty-three when I had my first real health scare. I was at Georgetown Hospital in Washington, going through a routine physical exam. While a nurse was measuring my blood pressure, I was making mental lists of the things I had to get done that day. The doctor was in, then out, then in again. At some point it occurred to me that she was speaking with unusual seriousness. She finally caught my attention with the word *lump*.

Here was the downside in my philosophy of assuming the best until told the worst: I had actually noticed the lump and assumed it was just a harmless cyst. It had happened before. No problem. But now I was hearing the worst, things like "biopsy" and "surgery," and how the lump would not "aspirate," and how it had to "come out" right away.

I felt myself beginning to black out and asked if I could lie down on the examination table while my doctor explained what all this meant. As if through a thick fog, I heard her talking about how long it took to get lab results after surgery and about how she always liked her patients to come to the office to review the results and "discuss alternatives." Suddenly, my day — or what I thought was going to be my day — had changed radically. My deadlines disappeared, and my priorities were dramatically re-arranged.

A week after the surgery, we got the results. The lump was benign. But what a long week that had been, full of what-ifs. I learned how easily big fears in life can wipe out the small ones. All the petty clashes and trivial disagreements disappear when the recognition of what *really* matters suddenly flares up. Moments of high intensity, of sickness and thoughts of death, are moments when God taps us on the shoulder and reminds us of the impermanence of things we assume are always going to be there — people, relationships, the future — and the value of all we take for granted. There's nothing like the prospect of losing something to make us realize what it's really worth.

Even those of us who are in enviable shape are not immune to fears of impending illness. For Lynda Resnick, the mastermind behind the pomegranate juice Pom Wonderful, the online florist Teleflora, and the revamping of Fiji Water, it's a chronic phobia (albeit one she can joke about). "I learned I was a hypochondriac way before I could spell it. Eventually I accepted that a headache wasn't necessarily the first sign of a brain tumor, and a little chest pain probably wasn't a heart attack but the result of a pepperoni pizza. But the fear is always there, as omnipresent as . . . *germs.* Going for my annual checkup still gives me palpitations."

When illness actually strikes, fear compounds the painful reality. Arlene Hogan, the headmistress of the Archer School for Girls in Los Angeles, had an unexpected open-heart surgery in her forties: "Being suddenly so completely incapacitated by open-heart surgery was terrifying. Despite reassurances from my surgeon that heart repairs were fairly tried-and-true procedures, I knew how high the physical stakes were and was completely overwhelmed at the possibility of a very altered life. Recovery, both physical and mental, was extraordinarily difficult. Things had gotten more complicated than I had anticipated, and I was languishing in a depressing hospital room for nearly two weeks. On day twelve, I fell apart, sobbing to my sister that I couldn't take it anymore. Her reply was to tell me I was my mother's daughter: 'You're just like Mom. You're a survivor.'"

Now Arlene is able to help other women face the fear of open-heart surgery, and as a result of her own experience, her life has become more of a celebration than it ever was before: "Each morning, I remind myself that I'm one of the really lucky ones. I'm still alive. I'll get to feel the breath in my lungs, the sun on my face, and, yes, hear the beat of my own heart (these titanium valves are noisy little things!)."

ON BECOMING FEARLESS ABOUT AGING AND ILLNESS

One thing we all share is that we can't escape aging. Since old age is unavoidable (hopefully), the only question that remains is how we deal with it — and what we choose to do with our lives in the meantime.

It's helpful to put our fears into perspective. For one thing, our culture's concept of aging — treating it like a disease to be fought with everything we have — isn't universal. It's learned. Which means it can also be unlearned. In fact, I'm lucky enough to have come from a country that honors and reveres old age.

Ten years ago I visited the monastery of Tharri on the island of Rhodes with my children. There, as in all of Greece, abbots are addressed by everyone as "Geronda," which means "old man." Abbesses are called "Gerondissa." Not exactly terms of endearment in my adopted home. The idea of honoring old age, indeed identifying it with wisdom and closeness to God, is in startling contrast to the way we treat aging in America. The geronda at the Tharri monastery was not even old — he was probably in his late fifties. But "old man" and "old woman" are titles bestowed on older people because of the respect they inspire.

Honoring elders isn't confined to the Greeks, of course. It's part of most indigenous American traditions, such as the Inupiat of Alaska, who require not just respect for but deference to their elders, especially from children. Traditional Asian societies also give the highest social rank to their oldest members, in both the family and the community.

Even if you're not ready to consider yourself a fearless sage, remember that age definitely isn't what it used to be. It's not just that life expectancy is now so much greater in the industrialized world — it's gone up from the late forties in 1900 to nearly eighty in 2000 — it's also that our forties and fifties are now seen as prime years. Fifty really *is* the new thirty. And antiaging medical advances could further increase Americans' life expectancy — from eighty years old to one hundred by the year 2030.

THE UPSIDE OF AGING

In order to become fearless about growing older, we should know what to expect as time changes our bodies. This preparation can help us adjust to the changes with less apprehension.

And it's not all bad. Most of us know to anticipate hot flashes and drier skin with menopause. But there are other changes — in the female brain in particular — that we should look forward to.

Louann Brizendine's book *The Female Brain* explains how, beginning in midlife, due to changes in our hormone levels and brain chemistry, women start to care less about others' opinions and more about what matters to them. This is also the time when more women than men initiate divorce.

According to Brizendine, during childbearing years, a woman's brain is "programmed with a delicate interplay of hormones, physical touch, emotions, and brain circuits to care for, fix, and otherwise help those around her. Societally, she has always been reinforced to please others."

However, starting at perimenopause and continuing into menopause, women experience "a new constancy in the flow of impulses through their brain circuits. This replaces the massive surges and plunges of estrogen and progesterone caused by the menstrual cycle." The change also relieves "the urge to avoid conflict at all costs." We are witnessing what Brizendine calls "the Mommy Brain beginning to unplug." The happy consequence is that a lot more energy becomes available to us.

These hormonal and brain chemistry changes also coincide with a drop in testosterone (yes, we have it), which regulates our sex drive. For some women this means less interest in sex, but for others it prompts what anthropologist Margaret Mead called "postmenopausal zest" — and a greater desire for adventure and new beginnings. Not a bad trade-off for drier skin and hot flashes.

It's not just our emotions and our sex drive that change as our brain ages. Although our basic intellectual capacity doesn't change, our style of thinking does. "Older adults move toward a simpler and more direct style of writing or painting, for example, that is easier for other people to understand," according to Professor Carolyn Adams-Price, a member of the Gerontology Committee at Mississippi State University. It's good to know that we are wired for greater simplicity as we mature.

TAKING CARE OF THE BODY

While positive changes happen to our gray matter quite naturally all by themselves, there are many proactive steps we can take to remain as healthy and vibrant as we can while we're aging. We may not be able to slow the march of time, but we've learned a lot more about how to take care of ourselves before our time is up. After all, preventive health care has advanced by leaps and bounds — we just need to stop our busy lives long enough to educate ourselves about everything that's now possible.

I'm definitely not a doctor and I'm not going to give medical advice here, but I can speak from experience about the power of preventive health care, whether it's through mercury detox or a daily supply of antioxidants, fish oils, green teas, and organic meats, fruits, and vegetables.

In today's world, where thousands of chemicals are being used all around us, it's essential both to protect against exposure and to maintain some kind of detox program. There are many good books on detoxification; one I found particularly useful was *Detoxify or Die* by Sherry A. Rogers.

Soram Khalsa, MD, is a founding member of the American Holistic Medical Association and a passionate advocate of detoxification as central to delaying the effects of the aging process and reducing the likelihood of chronic degenerative diseases. When I started on Dr. Khalsa's detoxification program, I was stunned to find out how much mercury I had in my body. Getting rid of heavy metals and pesticides, he told me, is a long-term process, since the body stores these toxins not only in our blood but in our fat. As my body started to detoxify, the changes in my mental clarity and my energy level were so remarkable that I've made his detox program part of my regimen. I've given up tuna, halibut, and swordfish forever and I've grown to love infrared saunas and body wraps, the modern equivalent of a Native American sweat lodge; they draw out the toxins as I lie there sweating away. If you like multitasking as much as I do, you can leave one arm out and make phone calls.

As for our outermost layer, there are many antiaging skin care treatments we can use without having to resort to plastic surgery. Three years ago I was on a hike with Sherry Lansing, then head of Paramount, and I was marveling at her skin. I knew she was approaching sixty — she has always been open about her age — and had never had so much as a Botox injection. I asked her what the secret was. She told me about her amazing aesthetician, Mila Moursi, who specializes in women who don't want to go under the knife.

For my birthday Sherry gave me a gift certificate, and I've been hooked ever since. My regular facials at Mila's include microdermabrasion, a skin-freshening technique to help repair skin that's taken a beating from the sun and from aging. But even the simplest home facial can cleanse and freshen up our skin and our spirits, even if it doesn't erase our crow's-feet. And when we feel better about ourselves, we are less fearful about aging.

FINDING STRENGTH IN TIMES OF ILLNESS

Preventive care is always important, but as we age, the chances increase that illness may strike, hard and unexpectedly. And sometimes even after we recover from the illness, we are filled with fears about getting back into life. Diana Meehan, founder of the Archer School for Girls, has always been physically fearless. She describes herself as someone who "used to walk on my hands across the top bar of the swing set and leap across a mountain chasm rather than walk around it." So it was quite a blow when, struck with a debilitating autoimmune disease, she was relegated to the couch in her living room for most of her waking hours.

"When I began to recover," she told me, "I had to learn to walk, reach, and raise my arms as if I'd never done it." Swimming and kayaking still seemed impossible. Then "one glorious spring Sunday when the Pacific Ocean was almost pacific, my brother Tom and his sons got the two kayaks out, and I had a rush of emotion seeing the bright-colored vessels on the beach pointed toward the water. 'Will you go with me?' I asked Tom. In high school he'd been a surfer and a lifeguard, so he knew I was asking if he thought I could do it." She did it, and it helped her overcome her fear "of being physically restricted, restrained by gravity or gender or age from leaping into the unknown."

At other times, we need to adjust to the permanent changes brought by illness. Gloria Berger, who happens to be Fran Lasker's mother and the grandmother of one of my daughter's best friends, talked to me about dealing with macular degeneration, a progressive eye disease: "I was deeply fearful of how I would handle this handicap. I thought that my life force was only as vital as my physical body. The thought of life without vision was devastating, and over these last five years I have had many moments where my world felt dark and lonely. But as time has gone on, I have discovered a new strength in myself and a new sense of accomplishment, as I have been challenged to go on with my life. I discovered that I'm able to continue sculpting by relying on my tactile sense. And I'm even able to continue dancing!"

DETOX THE SOUL — LETTING GO

Growing older fearlessly certainly requires maintenance of our bodies and adjusting to illness. But at least as important as the upkeep of our external selves is making sure we take care of our inner selves. Old hurts, angers, and resentments are as destructive to our spirit as mercury and pesticides are to our bodies. Staying in negative relationships can be more toxic than what we eat, drink, or inhale. Avoiding people who, for whatever reason, are not good for us is more and more important as we grow older. And with less sand left in the hourglass, letting go of what isn't working is crucial to overcoming the fear of aging.

On my fortieth birthday I made a list of all the things I was no good at, didn't enjoy, or had thought I might do one day but, realistically, were simply not going to happen. Far from depressing me, admitting these things to myself and getting rid of the anxiety of perpetually unmet expectations was actually extremely liberating.

That's how I gave up skiing. I was really bad at it and didn't enjoy it enough to put in the energy and time it would require (a lot) to get better. I wanted to enjoy it, as many of my friends genuinely seem to. But it was such a relief when I admitted to myself that I just didn't. That's also how I crossed learning German off my list. Yes, it would be nice to be able to speak German. But I was never going to have the time to do it. It was simply not a high enough priority.

Clearing out things — clothes, objects, equipment we no longer need or use — also gives us a freedom and clarity that are all the more important as we age. Books, especially underlined and highlighted and written-in books, are my challenge, constantly threatening to engulf me. When there are just too many of them piled up on the floor of my office, I take them to the garage and pile them up there instead. Not ideal, but I'm learning; at least they're getting farther away. Pretty soon, maybe I'll even take them off the property.

Letting go, shedding, simplifying — these are all hard to do in a culture built on addition rather than subtraction. But when we stop holding on to things we'll never use and stop struggling to be who we are not, we discover newfound energy and strength. It takes courage and conscious decision-making to do this. When we're younger, we define ourselves by our work, by our families, by a dozen external measures. But as we age and outgrow old roles, we can feel adrift, purposeless, and filled with fear — unless we focus on what's growing rather than what's dying. Since our cells change all the time, shouldn't our mental and emotional states be constantly regenerating, too? Mental stagnation is the fastest way to grow old.

FREE TO DREAM AT ANY AGE

When we start to let go of things that we're not passionate about, we're free to initiate new projects and pursue new passions. This is one of the best ways to become truly fearless about aging. I was fifty-two when I discovered the blogosphere and first wrote about it. Sixteen months later, I wrote about it again, confessing that "I've got a big-time crush. I'm talking weak-in-the-knees infatuation. But it's not Brad or Orlando or Colin or any of the cinematic hunks du jour who have set my heart aflutter. No, it's Atrios and Kos and Josh Micah Marshall and Kausfiles and Kevin Drum and Wonkette. Bloggers all. Yes, when it comes to the blogosphere, I'm a regular cyberslut. And I don't care who knows it." (For the record, I've gotten even cybersluttier.)

One year later, on May 9, 2005, we launched the Huffington Post. The Internet is supposed to be a young person's game, and, as expected, the launch was greeted by a cacophony of ill wishers. Nikki Finke, writing in the *LA Weekly*, went so far as to declare us dead on arrival. Within hours of our birth, she wrote, under the headline "Why Arianna's Blog Blows," that "the Madonna of the mediapolitic world has undergone one reinvention too many. She has now made an online ass of herself. . . . This website venture is the sort of failure that is simply unsurvivable. Her blog is such a bomb that it's the movie equivalent of *Gigli, Ishtar,* and *Heaven's Gate* rolled into one." Ouch. A simple "congrats" would have sufficed. (Interestingly, one year later, on our first anniversary, Nikki Finke described the Huffington Post as "an asset to the Internet dialogue. Today I can go on the site and see stories in one place that I can't find on mainstream news sites." And she e-mails us her stories to post on the site, which we are happy to do.)

I'm certainly not unique in launching a new project in my fifties. A 2005 *Time* magazine article poked a hole in the concept of the midlife "crisis," pointing out that later in life more women than men are jumping in and starting new projects: "36% of those between 50 and 64 reported that they had fulfilled a dream, compared with 24% of younger women and 28% of their male peers."

Of course, I had plenty of fears as I took my leap into the unknown, but I knew they were mostly just feeble echoes of earlier fears. I'd learned not to be afraid of my critics and would certainly never let them stop me. In fact, the most freeing thing about getting older is realizing how little power the naysayers have over us — unless we give it to them. The important thing isn't whether your new venture is a smashing success or a middling failure. The important thing is that you're doing it.

LEARN FROM THE GERONDISSA

Another key to aging without fear is to spend more time looking ahead and less time looking back — and definitely less time looking in the mirror. This isn't easy to do, but it certainly helps to find some older women in your life to serve as fearless role models. When I was twenty-four and on my first book tour, I was interviewed in Cleveland by fiery redhead Dorothy Fuldheim. She had begun her career as the news anchorwoman for WEWS-TV in Cleveland. She was eighty-one when she interviewed me and had been at the station since she was fifty-four — thirty-seven unbroken years. She had interviewed Albert Einstein and every president from Franklin Roosevelt to Ronald Reagan.

In 1970, after four Kent State University students were killed during a protest against the war in Vietnam, Dorothy went on TV and called it murder. There was so much opposition and so many letters objecting to her comments that she offered to resign. The station didn't accept her resignation, but the experience was like a baptism by fire and proved once more the adage that what doesn't kill you makes you stronger. Consumed by my own fears and anxiety, I was awed by how fantastically free and fearless Dorothy seemed. As I was traveling from city to city facing all the controversies about the "mommy wars" my book had provoked, I wondered whether I would have to get to my eighties before I could be as free and fearless.

Then there's Doris "Granny D" Haddock, a grandmother who in her late eighties spent fourteen months walking from the Pacific to the Atlantic to call attention to the desperate need for campaign finance reform. Many fearless women have fought for freedom; Rosa Parks sat for integration, and Granny D walked to restore our trust in our government. When she came to Los Angeles in the spring of 2000, my mother was still alive. I brought these two amazing women together and introduced Granny D to my daughters as a powerful example of how irrelevant age is when you are passionate about what you are doing. Granny D celebrated her ninetieth birthday by climbing the steps of the Capitol. "Democracy," she said, "is not something we have but something we do. It is my belief that a worthy American ought to be able to run for public office without having to sell his or her soul to the corporations or the unions. . . . Fund-raising muscle should not be the measure of a candidate."

Granny D proved her commitment to reform one step at a time with a lot of national publicity, but your role model doesn't have to be prominent — just fearless. In *Another Country*, Mary Pipher portrays the lives of many older people in the Midwest, including five beloved aunts — ordinary women whom she calls heroic for their individuality and coping skills. "The more we love and respect our elders," she writes, "the more we teach our children to love and respect us."

And the more older people Pipher interviewed for her book, the less scared she became of old age. It's when we segregate older people that we become afraid of the inevitable. We need to be in touch with the natural cycle of life and let our preoccupation with appearances fade as we become more engaged in causes larger than ourselves. That means spending more time with the gerondissas in our lives — our mothers, our neighbors, our aunts, our colleagues — listening to and learning from them.

I was blessed to have my own mother as my ultimate fearless role model. When she died, six years ago, I realized that she and I had been different in one key way: She lived in the rhythm of a timeless world, a child's rhythm; I lived in the hectic, often unnatural rhythm of the modern world. While I had the sense every time I looked at my watch that I was running out of time, she lived in a world where a trip to the farmers' market happily filled half a day, where there was always enough time for wonder at how lovely the rosemary looked next to the lavender. In fact, going through the market with her was like walking through the Louvre with an art connoisseur, except that you could touch and smell and taste the still lifes.

My mother embodied the qualities that we need to grow into as we grow older — especially simplicity and a connection with the sacred. For all those blessed to be in her orbit, it felt as if these dimensions of life were taken care of. I was already fifty when she was gone, and I knew that however difficult, inconvenient, even unnatural it felt at first, it was time for me to start living more as she had lived.

The last time my mother was upset with me was when she saw me talking with my children and opening my mail at the same time. She despised multitasking. She believed it was simply a way to miss life, to miss the gifts that come only when you give 100 percent of yourself to a task, a relationship, a moment. She was quite certain in her belief that many of our emergencies were actually manufactured.

While our goal at the beginning of life is to see what we can make of it, my mother used to say that as we grow older, the goal is to see what it can make of us. Well, she made of life a grand adventure — and it made of her a magnificent tour guide, which is what many older people in our lives can become, if only we let them.

Whether you are twenty-five or seventy-five, you can channel your own inner gerondissa. Why not find a younger woman to mentor? It could be a student, a coworker, a neighbor. It could, of course, be your own daughter — on those blissful occasions when she's open to her mother's accumulated wisdom.

Rory Kennedy, filmmaker and youngest child of Robert Kennedy, told me how, as she grows older, "the larger issues — having children, my parents dying, the turbulence of life itself — come into focus, and one gets a sense of perspective about beauty and age. Overcoming obstacles and growing up require us to relinquish life's nonessentials and summon our energy to giving back to life. Facing the immensity of the universe and beginning to appreciate life's mystery, we find wisdom and feel an inner, transcendent beauty. Yes, we still wonder how we look and what to wear, but if we are lucky and no longer controlled by our many fears, we find a centered feeling that supersedes superficial worries."

The peace that eluded us in the middle of life's tumult when we were younger is one of our most sacred gifts as we grow older.

Sherry Lansing *on fearlessness*

I LIKE THE quote "There's a season for everything." I've always had this great fear that time would run out and life would have passed me by. I realized that I didn't want to die at my desk. I wanted to do something else and began to wonder: Am I defined by my job, and if so, what kind of a person am I? Is this really what I want to say with my life? Of course, I loved the movies and the movie business. I ran Fox for over three and a half years, produced movies for ten years, and then ran Paramount Pictures for over twelve years. I loved my job, but at a certain point it became repetitive. The highs weren't as high, and the lows weren't as low.

So I asked myself: What is it that really gives me pleasure? The answer is giving back. From the time I was twelve, I'd always been carrying these little tin cans around, trying to raise money for causes. I've always loved that kind of activism.

But it was a process — it took five years. I talked to everybody about it — to my husband, to my girlfriends, to my therapist, endlessly. I thought about the people I idolized — people like Jimmy Carter, Martin Luther King Jr. — and what they had done with their lives. And, in my teeny tiny way, I wanted to do what small part I could to follow in their footsteps.

I thought: What is my worst fear? Would I be bored? Would I have enough to do? Would I miss my job? I remember someone once asking me, "Will you regret not the things you did, but the things you didn't do?" So I concluded that I'd have no respect for myself if I didn't try to do something different. I thought, What's the worst that can happen? If it's a mistake, okay, I'll go back and make movies; you are allowed to change your mind.

Somewhere in my midfifties I realized that I was seeing a line of sorts — and that line was sixty. So, with sixty looming, I did it. It just felt right. I knew it was the right time, and so I retired from the entertainment business and committed myself to a career in philanthropy.

I formed my own foundation dedicated to cancer research and education. I serve on the board of the Carter Center and the California Institute for Regenerative Medicine, which disburses $3 billion in funds for stem cell research. I am a regent of the University of California and chair of its Health Services Committee. With my partner, Civic Ventures, I'm starting a movement, Prime-time, for those sixty and older to retire and give something back to the community. The funny thing is that I'm busier than I've ever been.

My advice on overcoming fears is to prepare for them. Talk about your fears — with your friends, your family, or in therapy, which I believe in. And then confront them. You don't have to do it fast, but once you've done it in your head, once you've visualized the worst-case scenario, it becomes easier to put one foot in the water and then the other.

I honestly can tell you that this is the happiest time of my life. It doesn't take anything away from what I was before; I still love movies, I still love my old friends. But now I have so many new friends, and I'm constantly learning new things. The big difference is that I control my own days and set my own agenda; I don't do anything that I don't want to.

I was in Paris recently and went for a walk in the Tuileries. I've probably walked through the Tuileries twenty times in my life. But I realized it was the first time I'd ever been there without a cell phone attached to my ear. It was a moment of pure joy. And I realized how lucky I was to have given it to myself.

Sherry Lansing serves on the board of the California Institute for Regenerative Medicine and was chairman and CEO of Paramount Pictures' Motion Picture Group.

$\mathscr{F}$earless About God and Death

Winning the Ultimate Endgame

WHY DO WE fear death? Most of us would probably agree with children's advocate Cheryl Saban: "My fear of death," she told me, "is connected first to pain, and to loss of someone I love, and the unknown, and then to the uncertainty about what my next adventure will be."

Clearly, it's not just that we fear no longer being able to do the things we do in our daily life on this side of the River Styx. As much as most people hate the thought of not seeing their grand-children grow up, or missing the season finale of *The Sopranos,* or not finding out whether the Red Sox or the Yankees will win the pennant, our fear is about what's on the other side, of what is ahead of us. For many, that means anticipating an encounter with some version of God. Will he be the wrathful God of the Old Testament? Will it be an eye for an eye, a tooth for a tooth? The day of judgment? The torments of hell?

In Christianity, the angry God of the Old Testament is super-seded by the God of love and forgiveness of the New Testament.

But millions of Christians — to say nothing of millions of Muslims, Hindus, Buddhists, Jews, and other faithful — still imagine God and the great unknown beyond this life as something utterly terrifying.

Many of us fear death because from an early age we are inculcated with the image of a vengeful God — an all-powerful being we both need and fear. Rama Fox, a real estate agent in Los Angeles, is one whose fears about death centered on this merciless version of God. "As a child I was taught in Sunday school to fear God. I was told God was all powerful, saw and knew everything, was jealous, wrathful, and punishing, although he did spare from eternal hellfire those who obeyed him. In my childlike heart I did not take this at all lightly. I was horrified that God, who knew everything and made everything, could punish me by having me burn in hell. To me, God was more demonic than divine, and I felt that only by fluke and provided I obeyed would I be spared because I knew about Jesus and had been baptized."

There are millions of people who believe in a wrathful God who punishes all those who haven't accepted his son as their savior — including those who never even had the chance to accept him. And Islam is similarly exclusionary. "They only are the believers whose hearts feel fear when Allah is mentioned," says a passage from the Koran. This exclusivity at the heart of much of organized religion only increases our fear and makes us unable to honor the common spirit within all people.

FEAR OF THE VAST UNKNOWN

When God is viewed as our great adversary, as was the case with Picasso (to whom the battle was more of a rivalry between two colleagues), we sublimate our fears into work, drugs, sex, television, alcohol, or some other addiction. And we align ourselves with people who can become our coconspirators in this tragic game of hide-and-seek — of trying to smother God and spirit and our fear of both with decidedly earthly distractions.

In Picasso's case, his main coconspirator in overcoming his fear of death at the end of his life was his last wife, Jacqueline. He threw himself into work, and while he was busy with work, Jacqueline was busy with him. Which meant making sure that everyone around him was complicit and on message, always reminding him that he was "more sprightly than ever," that he, alone in the world, would somehow cheat death. Even the press obliged. On his ninetieth birthday on October 25, 1971, there was this hubristic headline in *Le Figaro:* "Picasso will be 100 years old in 10 years."

Philosophers and religious teachers have been warning against this way of living for centuries. Socrates taught that we should "practice death" daily, to help us realize what's really important and evaluate the lesser in life in terms of the greater.

But our culture makes this harder than ever, intent as it is on practicing the denial of death. Our obsession with work or fun or shopping or those American Idols are ultimately just defensive strategies to fend off the fear of the unknown ahead. With Picasso, work became his shield, his talisman. It was work at the expense of everything — including good work. "I do worse every day," he said in a rare moment of self-awareness. But he did not let that stand in his way: "I have to work. . . . I have to keep going." Or . . . what, exactly? He didn't get that far in his introspection. Nor, of course, did his constant work keep him "going" forever.

FEAR OF FAITH

In the twentieth century, the response to fear-filled religiosity has been atheism and fear-filled alienation from all things spiritual. *Alienation* may be a sixties word, but it's by no means a sixties concept. It is, after all, just a name for that basic, atavistic feeling of not being "at home" in the world, a kind of cosmic homesickness. It was not born in the twentieth century, but it was certainly fed by existential philosophy and the denial of the existence of God.

Jean-Paul Sartre celebrated this terrible emptiness: "Life has no meaning. . . . It is up to you to give it a meaning, and value is nothing but the meaning that you choose." As the philosopher William Barrett puts it, "Sartre's atheism states candidly . . . that man is an alien in the universe, unjustified and unjustifiable, absurd in the simple sense that there is no . . . reason sufficient to explain why he or his universe exists."

Wow, if I thought that was the whole truth about our universe, I'd be pretty alienated and afraid and bummed out, too. And no amount of Sartre and intellectual muscle-flexing would assuage my fears. Engaging in nonstop activity so I didn't have to think about it would at least push my fear to the background. But I wouldn't be getting rid of it — only masking it.

Sometimes the fear manifests as an anxiety that hangs over us, one that we cannot ascribe to any particular cause or event. "Free-floating anxiety" is the term used by modern psychology, and by naming what we cannot explain, by classifying the symptoms, we delude ourselves into thinking we have somehow mastered the cause. Many years ago I read a column by a successful playwright recounting a day in his life that would be the envy of many, full of people and color and action and fun. I no longer remember his name, but his last line was burned into my brain: "I go to bed every night feeling that I have forgotten something." The nagging sensation of having forgotten something important, which disturbs our comfort and routine, both feeds our fear and is a product of it.

So for many the price of escaping from the prison of damnation-drenched religious conventions has been to lose touch with the spiritual truths from which they originally sprang. When that happens, our new reality is the fear-filled and barren terrain of sterile secular humanism. It's a false world in which the spiritual either gets taken over by fanatical fundamentalism or explained away by psychoanalysis as the residue of a damaged childhood. Indeed, one of Freud's most famous books about religion is entitled *The Future of an Illusion.*

Without faith in a higher order and the existence of something outside ourselves and our everyday lives, life can become emotionally unbearable and filled with fear. And this anxiety, even if we're not aware of it, will surface in other parts of our lives. Bernard Levin described it as "the gnawing feeling that ultimate reality lies elsewhere, glimpsed out of the corner of the eye, sensed just beyond the light cast by the campfire, heard in the slow movement of a Mozart quartet, seen in the eyes of Rembrandt's last self-portraits, felt in the sudden stab of discovery in reading or seeing a Shakespeare play thought familiar in every line."

But we spend a large part of our lives barricading ourselves against this ultimate reality. In the nineteenth century, Nietzsche called himself "a man who wishes nothing more than daily to lose some reassuring belief, who seeks and finds his happiness in this daily greater liberation of the mind." But the freedom he was seeking, which was essentially the freedom from fear and convention, cannot be found through the mind, only through the soul.

FEAR OF LOSS

For years I had longed to have children, so I was over the moon when, at thirty-six, I discovered that I was pregnant. But night after night, I had restless dreams. Night after night I could see that the baby — which I was sure was a boy — was growing within me, but his eyes would not open. Days became weeks, and weeks turned into months. Early one morning, barely awake myself, I asked out loud, "Why won't they open?" Michael turned and looked at me. "The baby won't open his eyes," I said. I knew then what was only later confirmed by the doctors. The baby's eyes were not meant to open; he died before he was born.

All I wanted to know was why? After five months of living in my womb, my baby had been born dead. "Why?" I asked of the nurses, of anyone, of no one, of God. For five months my heart had swelled with love as my belly had swelled with new life. How was I to know that I had cradled my child in his grave?

Women know that we do not carry our unborn babies only in our wombs. We carry them in our dreams and in our souls and in our every cell. Losing a baby brings up so many unspoken fears: Will I ever get pregnant again? Will I ever be able to give birth to a healthy child? Everything felt broken inside. As I lay awake during the many sleepless nights to come, I began to sift through the shards and splinters, hoping to find reasons. Gradually I began to realize that the answers would come in God's time, not mine.

Staggering through this minefield of hard questions and partial answers, I began to make my way toward healing. Dreams of my baby gradually faded, but for a time it seemed as if the grief itself would never lift. My mother had once given me a quotation from Aeschylus that spoke directly to these hours: "And even in our sleep, pain which cannot forget falls drop by drop upon the heart, and in our own despair, against our will, comes wisdom to us by the awful grace of God." At some point, I accepted the pain falling drop by drop and prayed for the wisdom to come.

I had known pain before. Relationships had broken, illnesses had come, death had visited people I loved. But I had never known a pain like this one. What I learned through it is that we are not on this earth to accumulate victories, things, and experiences, but to be whittled and sandpapered until what's left is who we truly are. This is the only journey that can get us to fearlessness, particularly in the face of pain and loss.

When I got pregnant again, I was constantly looking for signs that the baby was in trouble. I was terrified of losing this baby, too. But Christina arrived perfectly healthy, and my fears turned to ineffable joy, a joy that brought with it a spiritual experience I'll never forget.

I lay in bed nestling her to me for hours. When I finally grew sleepy, we put her in a crib next to my bed. A few moments later, after everyone had left the room, I began trembling convulsively. I tried to calm myself with the same soothing words I had just offered to my baby: "It's all right . . . it's all right."

And then my body was no longer shaking. I had left it. I was looking down at myself, at Christina, at the tuberoses on the nightstand, at the entire room. I had no fear at all; I knew I would return. And I was awash in a sense of enormous well-being and strength. It was as if a curtain had been pulled back to give me a glimpse of wholeness — birth, life, and death. Seeing them all at once, I could accept them all. For I don't know how long, I hovered in that state of almost tangible fearlessness and peace. Then I watched a nurse enter the room, and as she touched me, she jolted me back into the hospital reality. I returned with a great sense of confidence and joy. The fear and anxiety of taking Christina home had disappeared. I knew we would be fine.

Sometimes the fear of loss and of pain makes us avoid risks by staying away from love, by not giving of ourselves, by living in a defensive way. "Emotional detachment is one such defense," Judith Viorst writes in *Necessary Losses*. "We cannot lose someone we care for if we don't care." But then it's like living without flowers, because, as the husband of a friend of mine said, "Flowers are messy — their petals fall off, the water spills, and aside from that, they die!"

We may try to protect ourselves against our fear of loss with plastic flowers and lukewarm attachments, but we won't be living a fully realized life.

ON BECOMING SPIRITUALLY FEARLESS

Our conventional way of thinking about the world remains profoundly dualistic. The physical and the rational in a supposedly eternal and inexorable battle against the unseen and the spiritual. In fact, the barriers between these two dimensions — built by the narrow rationalism of the Enlightenment — are now being dismantled by modern science and a growing chorus of personal experiences. What we're seeing — if we are willing to look — is that we are not alone in an indifferent universe. As Goethe put it, "This life, gentlemen, is much too short for our souls." If this life were sufficient for our souls, we would not go through it consumed with fear.

Reintegrating the spiritual and the everyday is the key to fearlessness. But ending this division is not easy when we've stopped even acknowledging that we live caught between these two worlds. When we're consumed with climbing the career ladder or just making a living, the spiritual seems unreal and far away. So we keep it conveniently penciled in one day a week, we seek it out only in moments of crisis, or we deny it altogether while trying to convince ourselves that we can overcome all fears and obstacles on our own.

Which is not to say we're not religious. Seventy percent of Americans belong to a religious organization and 40 percent of adults attend services once a week. "The downside to all this," writes Jeffrey Kluger in his 2004 *Time* article "Is God in Our Genes?" "is that often religious groups gather not into congregations but into camps — and sometimes they're armed camps. . . . Why then do we so often let the sweetness of religion curdle into combat? The simple answer might be that just because we're given a gift, we don't necessarily always use it wisely."

Here's the bottom line: If you believe in a God who only judges and punishes, or if you believe that there is nothing but an accidental, indifferent universe, it's going to be incredibly hard to move from fear to fearlessness because, after all, the essential characteristic of fearlessness is trust. It's the trust that there is meaning in our lives, even when our limited minds are unable to see it, the trust that's captured in one of my favorite verses in the Bible: "Not a sparrow falls but that God is behind it."

The alternative is a pessimism and an impatience that despair of life and seek hope either in the end of the world or in worldly panaceas.

BEING AND *SOMETHING*NESS

When we tap into the truth that we are spiritual as well as material beings, we are then able to distinguish between our transient day-to-day concerns and that which is eternal and immutable. Understanding which is which helps us overcome our fears, not just our fears of God and dying but our fears of loss.

What form the spiritual takes is up to you. I was raised Greek Orthodox, but what Will Durant said about Catholicism applies to the Greek church too: "The worship of Mary transformed Catholicism from a religion of terror — perhaps necessary in the Dark Ages — into a religion of mercy and love." It was indeed the spirit of the Virgin Mary that moved and comforted me when I was a girl. Whenever I felt alone and afraid, I prayed to Mary. When schoolyard squabbles broke out, when my sister grew quiet and sick, when my father moved away and didn't come home, I prayed to Mary.

She went with me to England and into adulthood. From the tumult of the debating chamber at Cambridge to the quiet of my first apartment in London, she was there. When I moved to a new homeland in New York, when I miscarried, when I divorced, at every fearful, difficult moment in my life, I looked to Mary as a spiritual guide.

But I also looked to the powerful archetypes in my beloved

Greek mythology for guidance in my life — especially to the goddess Hestia. Hestia is the goddess of the hearth, the eternal center to which life returns to be replenished — a gathering point that's always there providing security in a chaotic world. Her name means "the essence of things," and since she is the essence of everything that moves and flows and has life, she was worshipped in ancient Greece as the center of the home, of the city, of the world.

But even more than comfort and centeredness, Hestia represents the bedrock of our being. She is not about striving and straining, competing and succeeding; she is all about "being." As Carl Jung put it, Hestia manifests "the almost irresistible compulsion and urge to become what one is, just as every organism is driven to assume the form that is characteristic of its nature." With gods like this, how did Greek mythology lose out? (At least our invention of democracy took off.)

Then there is my favorite god: Hermes. He embodies both serendipity and that which never changes. Whenever things seem fixed, rigid, stuck, Hermes introduces fluidity, motion, new beginnings. He was the god who first gave me, as a child, a sense of the miraculous all around me. Introducing the element of the unexpected into our lives is one of the means he uses to spur us out of our complacency, to break through the inertia and confinement of habit and convention.

Hermes represents a very important key to fearlessness: the freedom of not having to be in control all the time, of not always having to be the one who makes things happen. His dual nature also helps us accept life's great paradox: that the only constant is change. Which is why he is the god of connections, bridging realms and dissolving frontiers between earth and the under-world, men and gods, life and death.

You don't have to be Greek to benefit from the wisdom of the Greek gods. Nor do you have to wait until you get to the other side to experience Hestia's and Hermes' essence. The ability to bridge the gap between ourselves and that something greater than ourselves is available to us at all times. It's the bridge be-tween what we know and what we only dimly perceive, between what we are now and what we can become.

As we start to walk across that bridge, as we make that con-nection, we gain perspective on our lives. When, between high school and college, I studied comparative religion at Shantini-ketan University, founded by Rabindranath Tagore, outside Cal-cutta, I learned a lot about the Shinto form of Buddhism centered on mindfulness. Through the simple act of paying careful atten-tion — whether to what we eat, how we move, or where our thoughts wander — we become aware of the significance our minds attach to things. And in that awareness, we recognize how intercon-nected everything is. All religions have similar practices that can free us from the fear that results from the need to control. As Hermes teaches us, it is so freeing simply to let go and trust.

YOU ARE HARDWIRED FOR THE SACRED

The instinct for spirituality is hardwired in us. This is our fourth instinct, the one beyond the instincts of survival, power, and sex. It is a genetically based, physical instinct that has a metaphysical purpose. It is a natural hunger for supernatural sustenance. It propels us to find meaning and transcend our mundane selves. It is the rejection of a false duality and the acceptance of the wholeness that is our true nature.

Scientific evidence now exists that shows how the fourth instinct works. "Even among people who regard spiritual life as wishful hocus-pocus," *Time*'s Jeffrey Kluger writes, "there is a growing sense that humans may not be able to survive without it. . . . The need for God may be a crucial trait stamped deeper and deeper into our genome with every passing generation. Humans who developed a spiritual sense thrived and bequeathed that trait to their offspring. Those who didn't risked dying out in chaos and killing." Just as fear has an evolutionary purpose, so does spirituality.

This is also the thesis of *The God Gene: How Faith Is Hardwired into Our Genes,* by molecular biologist Dean Hamer. "Human spirituality," Hamer says, "has an innate genetic component to it. It doesn't mean that there's one gene that makes people believe in God, but it refers to the fact that humans inherit a predisposition to be spiritual — to reach out and look for a higher being."

Jung clearly understood the critical nature of our spiritual instinct. He was adamant that among his patients thirty-five years and older, "there has not been one whose problem in the last resort was not that of finding a religious outlook on life. It is safe to say that every one of them fell ill because he had lost what the living religions of every age have given to their followers, and none of them is really healed who did not regain his religious outlook. This, of course, has nothing to do with a particular creed or membership in a church."

So if we're still living in a state of existential fear, it's likely that we've lost our spiritual outlook. We haven't yet tapped into our "God gene." Or, put still another way, we haven't yet started living from our fourth instinct. Fear, after all, is a form of atheism, an emotional rejection that anything greater than our small, temporal, temporary selves exists.

"Ask your soul!" pleads Hermann Hesse in *My Belief.* "Your soul will not blame you for having cared too little about politics, for having exerted yourself too little, hated your enemies too little, or too little fortified your frontiers. But she will perhaps blame you for so often having feared and fled from her demands, for never having had time to give her, your youngest and fairest child, no time to play with her, no time to listen to her song, for often having sold her for money, betrayed her for advancement. . . . You will be neurotic and a foe to life — so says your soul — if you neglect me, and you will be destroyed if you do not turn to me with a wholly new love and concern."

JOURNEY BEYOND THE EGO

Fearlessness, with the attendant characteristics of optimism, confidence, and hopefulness, is neither a blindness to suffering and tragedy nor a personal quirk that some have and some don't. Throughout the ages fearlessness has been the hallmark of spiritual thinkers refreshingly at odds with the worldview that sees us as accidental specks in a universe indifferent to our fates, living out meaningless lives, our evolution an aimless process of happenstance.

The moment we choose to look beyond the circumstances of our lives is actually the beginning of our spiritual journey. As we start to tap into the inner resources we all have available to us, we may initially also tap into new fears — fears that our current lifestyle, the one we're used to, the one we take for granted as the only possible one, may actually be threatened. We may fear looking foolish, being wrong, having prioritized the wrong things and having missed the most important ones. (The Greeks have a word for missing the mark: *amartia,* which, incidentally, translates as "sin.")

It turns out that the real fear of knowing God is a fear for our ego, which is built around all the things we think we are, tell others we are, and make believe we are.

If you have ever been around a person with Alzheimer's, you know it can be a profoundly humbling experience. Because it allows you to see that there is something in us beyond our egos, our minds, and our personalities. Bernard Levin, my first love who remained a lifelong friend, was struck by the disease in the 1990s. I had been with him at the beginning of the journey into this other world. It was 1988, when he had come to stay with me in Santa Barbara and we had made the round of doctors in Los Angeles to find out why he kept losing his balance and was not able to retrieve certain words. Looking back, I find it astonishing that nobody diagnosed it as early-stage Alzheimer's.

The hardest time for me — even more so for him, of course — was four years later. By then I was living in Washington, and he came to stay with me. The medium he had mastered — words — was now deserting him. When I last saw him, in London, shortly before he died, the Alzheimer's had advanced to the point where he had absolutely no recollection of me. We sat for tea, a favorite ritual of his. But no matter what memories, nicknames, or shared moments I brought up, there was no connection. Here was the man who had introduced me to the world's greatest literature, art, and opera, yet now I had the sense he was teaching me, in the most painful way, something much more profound — that even the most brilliant brain does not begin to define who we are. That even the most amazing accomplishments are only a small part of who we are.

It was such a cruel lesson. The man who could recite lengthy passages from Shakespeare without faltering was now struggling to find a simple, everyday word lost in the recesses of his memory.

"I fell to speculating," he once wrote, "about what it would be like to be a prisoner in reality instead of fantasy, and came to the astonishing and disturbing conclusion that provided I could read and write what I liked, and had a congenial cell-mate (or better still, a sentence of solitary confinement), I would not find it nearly so terrible as I surely ought to." These things were now denied him, yet there was a presence about him that was soulful and beyond anything I had ever seen in him — as though his brilliance and his accomplishments were no longer masking his essence.

I have heard others recount similar experiences. It's as if when the mind is gone, something else shines through, something that was blocked by the churning factory of the intellect. So, just as people find new life in physical illness, their spirit can find new life beyond the mind.

FINDING THE PATH TO GRACE

Ultimately, to reach fearlessness and overcome our fear of death, we need to bring into our daily lives a grace beyond our minds and our emotions. There is no better way to do this than with a daily practice. As the Quakers say, "When you pray, move your feet." And when you move your feet, you can pray.

When I feel disheartened by all that's going on in the world around me, I turn to the profound truth Gandhi gave expression to: "I have found that life persists in the midst of destruction. Therefore there must be a higher law than that of destruction. Only under that law would well-ordered society be intelligible and life worth living."

One way I remind myself of the need to translate Gandhi's spiritual truth into my daily life is by keeping in a little frame on my desk a saying that I also like to give my friends on their birthdays: "If you do your 10 percent 100 percent, God will do the 90 percent and you'll live in grace." Once we recognize that even when we put everything we have into a project or a relationship, many factors beyond our control determine the outcome, a lot of the stress and fear evaporate. And we can live in grace.

And there are so many ways for us to bring more peace and spirit into our 10 percent. My mother introduced my sister and me to yoga when I was twelve years old. Her belief in God was much more than church on Sundays. When we were teenagers, she taught us how to meditate. It wasn't something I took up regularly when I was thirteen, but many years later I realized that she had planted a seed that would become a very important part of my life: the notion that quiet time before the world starts spinning is crucial both to nourishing the soul and to being effective in the world.

Meditation, yoga, affirmations, and daily prayer all help connect us to this higher reality beyond our immediate concerns.

My mother even made washing the dishes part of her spiritual practice (though, hard as she tried, she was never able to make vacuuming play that role!). The payoff for spiritualizing the everyday is immediate and enormous. When we look at our world from a higher point of view, all our fears are put into perspective and even our biggest problems become less intimidating.

THE STUFF OF DREAMS

One thing that can help bring timelessness into our lives is rediscovering the sacred in the most mundane and often the most resented ritual of our day: sleep. Insomnia can just be the stubborn refusal of our hyperactive minds to surrender to a temporary nonexistence and yield control for a few hours.

Some years ago, I visited the "sleeping chambers" in Egyptian temples, chambers to which initiates would retire after they had prepared, through prayer and meditation, to receive in sleep divine guidance and inspiration. In stark contrast to the modern habit of drugging ourselves senseless, hoping to "crash" for a few hours before having to face another frantic day, the Egyptians went to sleep expectantly. So sleep was not only a time of rest but of regeneration. From my own experience, I've noticed that when I prepare spiritually for sleep by playing a meditation tape or even by saying a simple prayer, I'm more likely to access remnants of my dreams and memories from my night's travels.

Dreams show us how much exists beyond our conscious mind. They have their own logic, their own vocabulary. They are like visits from the great beyond. As we connect to our dream world, we connect to a source far greater than even the most brilliant minds.

MEMENTO MORI

The ancient Romans used to carve *MM* on the bases of statues and on the trunks of trees. The letters stand for *Memento Mori:* Remember Death. This was not intended as a sign of morbidity but as a mental tool with which to overcome the fear of the unknown, a way to come to terms with life's only inevitability, demystifying it by keeping it close. Remembering death, reminding ourselves of its silent presence, can help us appreciate life to the fullest.

Rory Kennedy's father, Robert Kennedy, was assassinated six months before she was born. So death has been part of her life from the very beginning. "We're all one breath away from not being here," she told me. "I've tried to use my father's death and many untimely passings in my family as ways to remember how precious life is, and to try to embrace every moment and every second of it, as opposed to living in fear that something horrible might happen. Because indeed something horrible *might* happen, but all we can do is be grateful for the time we have here and make the most of it."

Trusting that there is more to the world than what we can see and finding a way to connect to it can help us face our mortality with fearlessness and bring this fearlessness to our everyday life.

Agapi Stassinopoulos on fearlessness

WHEN I WAS ten, my parents separated. I was devastated. My world collapsed, and with it the vibrant, joyful, and exuberant girl I had been. It would take me a long time to recover from the loss.

My survival mechanism was to try and get some control over my disintegrating reality by building an image of perfection and hiding all the pain behind it. I even created a fictional character called Anna. She was independent, strong — a Greek Pollyanna — and kept me going. I might have been vulnerable and full of fear, but my best friend, Anna, was cool and fearless.

At seventeen I moved to London to study at the Royal Academy of Dramatic Arts. I loved acting, but the real me was still relating to the world through this mask, aching to feel more deeply connected to life and to others.

I was excited when I got a part for a movie in Los Angeles. And all the more disappointed when it fell through. I was given a return ticket to London but didn't use it. It was a huge risk on my part, but it led me on a journey of soul searching. I started doing hours of Bikram yoga, using my body and my breathing and movement to break through the straitjacket of trying to be perfect. I started meditating and read dozens of spiritual books. Then one morning while I was meditating, a veil was lifted and my spirit opened up. Call it grace. In an instant I felt an inner connection to the self I had so masterfully tucked away after my parents' separation. That strong and vibrant girl was still there, intact under the layers of protection. Now my false self-image was busted, and for the first time, bathed in the light, I wasn't alone and I wasn't afraid.

I had *me*. I was getting *me* back and I knew that I had the resources to go through the ups and downs of life finally connected to the lifeline of my spirit and my inner strength.

I then understood that Agapi — the name I was given, which is Greek for "love" — was a gift reminding me that whatever the conditions of my life, I could always source my unconditional loving and find myself living in grace. Because, as Shakespeare wrote, love "is an ever-fixed mark, / That looks on tempests and is never shaken."

Agapi Stassinopoulos is an author and motivational speaker.

ℱearless About Leadership and Speaking Out

The Power of One

IN 2003, I ran for governor of California, part of a large field of candidates that included then Lieutenant Governor Cruz Bustamante and the ultimate victor, Arnold Schwarzenegger. As exhilarating as the experience was, it also had its bruising moments. None more so than the big televised debate Arnold dubbed "the Super Bowl of debates" (perhaps because it was the only one he took part in).

Throughout the debate, whenever I was making a point — indeed, whenever I opened my mouth — Bustamante, in his deep baritone, kept repeating, "Yes, Arianna. Yes, Arianna." Occasionally he would throw in an eye roll. It was a condescending refrain, weary and bored, as if he could barely summon the energy to tolerate a typical nagging woman. It was the equivalent of "Take two Midol and you'll feel better in the morning, honey."

Schwarzenegger expressed his displeasure at having to debate a full-throttle female by suggesting that I drink more decaf — a comment that is hard to imagine being addressed to a man.

In fact, that debate made me realize how deeply ingrained our culture's fear of assertive women is and how much of this fear women have unconsciously internalized. After the debate, I came off the stage and was immediately surrounded by dozens of young female students who thanked me for taking a stand and not backing down. I was moved by the gratitude — but also stunned by it. I certainly didn't think I deserved any special thanks simply for speaking my mind. Nor did I think that young women in 2003 would still be hungering for role models to help them gain the courage to find their own voice.

But even in 2006 it's hard for a woman to challenge prevailing orthodoxies and not be attacked and caricatured for it. We're still required, first and foremost, to be sweet and adorable. A man who doesn't toe the line is not only tolerated but even hailed as an appealing scamp or rogue, but an unconventional, self-assured woman is far more likely to be seen as a ball-busting bitch . . . who needs to drink more decaf.

Let's face it: Our culture still isn't comfortable with powerful, visible, outspoken women. We equate power with maleness, manliness, dominance — even ruthlessness — all of which happen to be traits that women fear being identified with because we know we will be called "pushy," "shrill," and "strident." The epithets strike right at our femininity — as if the very notions of power and womanliness are mutually exclusive. No wonder women are often afraid to stand up, take the lead, speak out. The result? A very uneasy relationship between women, power, and the traits necessary to be a leader.

But if we are going to tap into our natural reserves of leadership, and this means expressing ourselves without apology, we will need to move away from accepting these fear-driven stereotypes. "Fearlessness," wrote La Rochefoucauld, "is a more than ordinary strength of mind, which raises the soul above the troubles, disorders, and emotions which the prospect of great dangers are used to produce."

NOT YOUR FATHER'S IDEA OF LEADERSHIP

We tend to think of leadership solely as an external force — associated with those who effectively carry out the responsibilities of their office or direct their staff in a confident way. That's very useful, but it's only one kind of leadership. There is another kind — internal leadership — that does not depend on office or position or staff hierarchy or anything imposed or granted from without. This kind of leadership is generated instead by an inner force that compels us to try and make the surrounding world — whether it's our family, our community, the entire nation, or beyond — a better place.

"There comes a time," Martin Luther King said in 1968, "when one must take the position that is neither safe nor politic nor popular, but he must do it because conscience tells him it is right." King didn't wait for a leadership platform to be granted to him. It would have been a long wait. His leadership grew out of his moral authority and ability to inspire. He was the ultimate internal leader. And does anyone doubt that we're starving for such real leadership today, in a time when what passes for leadership means just being obsessed with finding the political middle, the elusive M-spot that, according to conventional wisdom, is the prerequisite for achieving power?

When we define leadership only in the most narrow, external way — thinking of it only as it relates to elected office and the executive suites of corporate America — we undervalue the internal qualities of leadership that made outsiders like Dr. King and Mahatma Gandhi and Mother Teresa such powerful leaders. For women to be fearless in leadership, they have to embrace these internal gifts.

There's no doubt that it takes some exceptional qualities to get to the top. Especially when on the way up, a woman will be dogged by charges of "ambition," "drive," and "pushiness." But the biggest obstacle isn't the media or male colleagues (or even some of our fellow females). Worse than the culture's approach to women in power are our own fears about power: the fear that we're setting ourselves up for attack, the fear that we'll alienate others, the fear that we may actually become the caricature of the obnoxious, shrill, she-devil boss. All these fears manifest themselves in the fear of expressing ourselves. It's an internalized censorship of ambition. Which is all the worse because, now more than ever, we need women leaders to take us beyond the world of fear we live in. Real leadership is too rare and too valuable to limit the pool to half the population.

The prevailing models of leadership today have been the leader as panderer or the leader as fearmonger, whipping up a climate of fear and then appealing to our most basic — and base — instincts. And following 9/11, we were all forced to add the fear of losing everything to terrorism to the garden-variety fears of losing our jobs, losing our health, losing a child to drugs, and so on.

But are we really any safer because of all the fear? Have we gained anything by it? More important, what have we lost? We need a new model of leadership, one that doesn't involve leading through fear but rather leading through bringing out what Lincoln called "the better angels of our nature."

As it turns out, women are ideally suited to supplying the qualities we need in leaders right now — being strong and decisive while at the same time being nurturing, wise, and respectful enough to tell the truth with a moral authority that inspires and empowers.

Soon after 9/11 and our invasion of Afghanistan, I saw *Harry Potter and the Sorcerer's Stone* — and a girl-power double feature began playing in my head. On one screen of my mental multiplex was the larger-than-life face of Hermione Granger, Harry Potter's fearless, brilliant, passionate, and dedicated partner in his battle against evil. On the other screen were the faces of the fearless Afghan women — members of the Revolutionary Association of Afghan Women (RAWA) — who battled against real-life villains whose savagery would tax even J. K. Rowling's fertile imagination.

Hermione is not your average schoolgirl. Besides being a bang-up wizard, the brightest student at Hogwarts, and a powerful female role model, she is also a modern manifestation of an ancient archetype embodied by Athena, the Greek goddess of wisdom and war. By following Athena's lead — and now Hermione's — women both young and old can learn to weave together strength and vulnerability, passion and discipline, intellect and imagination, and to breathe humanity and mercy into the masculine order. Which is what so many Afghan women have done against all odds.

The women of RAWA are not your average women, either. They are women like Soheila Helal, a teacher who defied the Taliban — and risked her life — by operating a clandestine school for girls; Kobra Zeithi, a pharmacologist-turned-activist who was imprisoned for the crime of traveling to Pakistan to pick up educational materials; and Weeda Mansoor and Tahmeena Faryal, who have tirelessly spoken out against the atrocities of the Taliban.

As Hermione and RAWA make clear, we can no longer afford to look for leadership solely among elected officials. We must learn to mine the greatest and most unexploited leadership resource available to us: ourselves.

FEAR OF SPEAKING OUT

Before women can lead, we have to confront one of our worst fears: speaking out in the world. Sure, many men are afraid of speaking out, too. But it's different for women. Nothing makes us more visible and therefore more subject to the criticisms specifically reserved for women in power. Every time we speak out, we might as well slap a target on our backs.

Yet it's impossible to be a leader if we're not willing to publicly stand up for what we believe. This is clearly a fear women have to learn to overcome. And I know from personal experience that it can be done.

I'm no longer afraid of expressing myself in public; in fact, I've come to enjoy it. But this was not always the case. I conquered this fear only because my love of politics and debate was stronger than my fear of criticism and failure. That old saying about love conquering fear turned out to be completely true in my case.

I owe my transformation to the Cambridge Union, the famed debating society at Cambridge. To say that I was afraid when I stood up to speak for the first time is like saying that Michael Jackson is a little quirky. My biggest fear was caused by my thick Greek accent — a not inconsiderable fear when you are trying to communicate and persuade. Would I be clearly understood? However, as I listened attentively to the sparring politicians in my first debate, I became convinced for the first time — though not the last — of the immense value of total incomprehensibility in public life.

I'd love to say that my first speech at the Union was one of those occasions when leaders are discovered and reputations born, but it wasn't. In fact, the chief clerk of the Union told me later that one of the secretaries, having listened to my speech, was overheard breathing a deep and very audible sigh of relief. "Thank God! At least I won't have to be typing that girl's funny name." Ah, sisterhood.

But I stuck with it. The apprenticeship had begun. Every Monday night became Union night. I would stay until the end and then wait to be called to speak. By this time, the only students left in the chamber were those whose inertia outweighed their judgment and those who had simply fallen asleep. But I loved watching the magic of people's minds moved by words. And as my desire to engage in the issues of the day grew stronger, my fear of being criticized for my funny name and funny accent began to wane.

In the second term of my first year I was given my big break. I was invited to propose the motion in a major debate. It was seconded by George Steiner, a brilliant writer and English professor, with guest speakers C. P. Snow and Lord Mountbatten opposing and Prince Charles, who was a student at Cambridge the same time I was there, speaking from what the Brits call the "crossbenches" — for neither one side nor the other.

The tension and drama in the packed house somehow made me less afraid, not more. Our side won the debate, and having one major speech and one victory under my belt greatly diminished my fears. I had done it once without mishaps. I could do it again — and better.

My Union life soon took an unexpected turn. While I was in London one weekend, Barbara Scott, a friend in her second year, put my name down in the candidates' book for the upcoming election for Standing Committee, which governed the Union. When I was given the news, I asked the chief clerk to withdraw my name. This was not a case of false modesty. It was a case of real fear: I was simply afraid that I would get no votes! Better not to run at all. But the ballots had already been printed. And, as it happened, I got enough votes to get elected.

Thus began my political life. And as I sat contemplating the election results — getting used to having actually been elected — the idea of becoming president of the Union first took root in my mind. I would like to say my ascendancy proceeded smoothly and courageously, but it didn't. Indeed, in my second year I so humiliated myself in a televised debate that I was convinced my Union career was over. The occasion was the debating equivalent of the Thrilla in Manila: J. K. Galbraith versus William F. Buckley. I was chosen to make the opening speech on Galbraith's side (against the free market, in case you're wondering). Galbraith spoke badly — very badly, in fact — and sat down beside me. Buckley, dripping smoothness, ease, and self-assurance, proceeded to tear him into elegant little pieces.

The professor was becoming visibly agitated. He leaned over and whispered in my ear, "Stand up and interrupt him — tell him that the conditions he's describing apply only to the stock exchange and that all other markets are far too imperfect to bear out his case." Um, perhaps. Maybe. But this was a debate, not a seminar. And Bill Buckley was a debating pro. But the venerable professor and Jeremiah of the "affluent society" was nudging me on. So I stood up, Buckley gave way, as tradition dictates at the Union, and I interjected. Then he coolly came back: "Madam, I do not know what market *you* patronize."

You may think that the Union had a strange sense of humor, but he brought the house down. I sat down with my cheeks burning and bid a silent farewell to the idea of ever holding another office at the Union. But a month later I had recovered sufficiently to attempt a comeback, speaking — with more success — alongside Bishop Trevor Huddleston and former defence secretary Denis Healey against the sale of arms to South Africa. At the end of term, I was elected secretary.

What I learned was that no one pays as much attention to our humiliations and defeats as we do. *I* may have thought my career was over, but others were not as focused on one devastating evening. The greatest unintended consequence for me was becoming less afraid of individual failures.

Lesson in hand, I threw my energies into Union life. Every

speech became a base camp for exploration. Some of my discoveries were totally useless for the actual debate but very useful for my education. As C. P. Cavafy, my favorite Greek poet, puts it, "Ithaca set you on the beautiful journey. / Without her you would never have taken the road." Gradually, the skeleton of what I believed began to emerge. As I became more passionate and serious about ideas, I became more fearless about expressing them. This included growing less fearful about publicly changing my views as I learned more about a subject — and dealing with the fallout. My Union experience would be critical to the rest of my life.

Had I not overcome the fear of public speaking and the fear of being publicly embarrassed and criticized, my whole career, indeed my whole life, would have been different. After all, it was becoming president of the Union that brought me to the attention of Reg Davis-Poynter, a British publisher, who offered me a book contract. It was an offer I accepted with trepidation. It set me on the path to becoming a writer, and meant that the Kennedy School of Government, where I had enrolled to go after Cambridge, became the road not taken.

ON BECOMING FEARLESS ABOUT SPEAKING OUT

Fearlessly expressing ourselves is a birthright we should cherish and take every opportunity to use. And the sooner we wade into these waters, the better.

Donna Bojarsky, now a public policy consultant, began her journey to master public speaking even earlier than I did — at thirteen. She describes her fears and how inspiring it was to overcome them: "There I was, about to become a bat mitzvah. . . . I loved rituals even then, so I was actually into the ceremony part even more than the party. I had chosen to expand my role in the service beyond what a child traditionally did. Now I regretted it deeply. Hundreds of people were there waiting . . . my family, school friends, large looming ark, big stained-glass windows. I was terrified.

"I looked at my mother with panic in my eyes, and tears started to well up. I couldn't do it. I wanted to run. But of course I couldn't, so I took a deep breath and started what felt like a mile-long walk up the stairs of the bimah — the dais. There was the microphone on top of the big, actually huge, podium where I was headed. I walked up the two big stairs and slowly looked out over the crowd. Trying to steady my knees and my nerves, I scanned all the familiar, expectant faces. Another deep breath. I started talking.

"And then something totally unexpected came over me, like a giant wave. I kept talking, surveying the congregation. Then I talked some more. Suddenly, *click*. A little surge ran through me. . . . This is really *fun*. . . . We *connect*, audience and me. This feels kind of *powerful*. . . . I *like* this!

"I remember that very moment as if it were yesterday. Even now, before I speak, that particular memory pops up, and I'm back in my wire-rimmed glasses and my granny dress . . . and I just smile to myself . . . and I start talking."

Achieving fearlessness in expressing our views is not a one-step process. Nor will it be a smooth journey without some deep potholes along the way. But I can say this: You'll never achieve it without taking that first step.

Stephanie Kang, an eleventh grader at the Archer School for

Girls, chose to join her debate team to get used to speaking out. "There was something about speaking in front of an audience that terrified me," she says. "I would constantly create excuses to avoid making speeches and was ambivalent about whether my ideas were smart enough or whether the audience would be receptive. I knew it was absurd, but I simply did not know how to get over it.

"Then I realized that it's all about taking risks and relying on impulse. How do I even know this fear is legitimate if I never take the opportunity to test it? Joining the debate team was a landmark for me. Throughout each debate, I would remind myself of the power and liberation of having and exercising a voice; and how I could not let a trivial fear squash that opportunity. This experience opened up a new window in my life — I was not a victim but a conqueror. My justifications for my fear were merely facades, and I began to believe in my capabilities."

Of course it's easy to move forward when things are going well, but it's when things are going badly or when we are challenging the status quo that it's most crucial to keep going.

That's what Jean Sara Rohe did at the New School 2006 graduation ceremony in New York. Rohe was one of two distinguished students invited by the faculty to speak to the graduates before Senator John McCain delivered his commencement speech. But when it was her turn to address the crowd, bravely and with dignity she announced that she was throwing out the prepared remarks she was going to make to address McCain directly, as she was disturbed by his support for the war in Iraq.

With the senator and likely 2008 presidential candidate seated just a few feet away, Rohe said, "The senator does not reflect the ideals upon which this university was founded," drawing cheers from the crowd. She went on to deliver an impassioned speech.

Can you imagine the courage that took? Not just to speak truth to power, but to do so in such a personal and public way?

Jean later blogged on the Huffington Post: "The entire afternoon leading up to my speech, I imagined that everyone who saw me knew what I was up to. I felt like an infiltrator. I wanted to go home and I was sick to my stomach. But eventually I spoke, and everyone loved it. . . . I never expected to get the opportunity to speak the way I did, but I'm so glad that I did. I hope that other people found strength in my act of protest and will one day find themselves in my position, drawing out their own bravery to speak truth."

UNLEASHING THE LEADER WITHIN

Fearlessness in presenting one's self and one's ideas to the world is a prerequisite to becoming a leader. It's hard to make a difference when you shrink from expressing who you are and what you stand for.

For Lonnae O'Neal Parker, author of *I'm Every Woman: Remixed Stories of Marriage, Motherhood, and Work,* this realization brought her face-to-face with many fears: "I used to play myself small. I reasoned it was enough to have occasional letters or articles or essays that would make a brief splash but leave ample time for me to scurry away behind my curtain, backstage where I could hide safely.

"Then I wrote an essay about race and identity and the personal as political history that generated sustained attention. I was asked to write a follow-up, I was asked to speak around the country, and, most unacceptably, I was asked to be on a prestigious news program. Just the idea turned flip-flops in my stomach. What if I was inarticulate? What if I rambled? What if I had fooled everyone and all the smart things they saw in me weren't really there at all? My backstage curtain beckoned and I longed to disappear, as I had always done, until all the fuss died down. But that is not what I did.

"This time, my shrinking felt corrupt. I had written an essay about black people with a lived history of being denied a voice while I had a voice and refused to raise it. I knew it would dishonor the ones who fought and struggled and came before me if I didn't find a way to transcend my fear. To represent. To speak my truth even when my voice quivers and my knees go weak. I understand deeply that there is simply no more time for women's silence on the urgent things of our day."

Empathy is an essential requirement of leadership — in large ways and small ones. I remember the evening that the results of the vice presidential election at the Cambridge Union were announced. Shirley Williams, who at the time was the leader of the Labour Party in Britain, was giving the Founders' Memorial Lecture at Girton College, my college at Cambridge. As secretary of the Junior Common Room, I had been invited to the dinner following the lecture and was seated next to Williams. She knew about the election taking place at the Union, and had it been an election involving her own Labour Party she could not have shown more concern.

During the dinner, someone finally came in and passed a piece of paper with the news that I had won to the Mistress of the College, our hostess for the evening. And Williams, who had understood my anxiety during the dinner, now shared my excitement. That evening solved for me the mystery of why she was one of the most popular politicians in Britain — across all parties. Her ability to empathize with someone else's hopes and fears and happiness — all of which I was feeling that night — was astounding. I saw clearly that part of being a fearless leader is the ability to recognize fear in others and help diminish it.

Empathy was a powerful attribute of the leadership of Eleanor Roosevelt, who used the role of First Lady as a platform from which to boldly speak out. She began life as a shy, awkward child, but when she came to the White House in 1933, she became a bold advocate for the poor, touring the country to witness for herself the effects of the Great Depression and speaking out at press conferences, at lectures, and in a daily newspaper column.

Following World War II and after FDR died in 1945, President Harry Truman appointed her to the first United Nations General Assembly. She was instrumental in developing the Universal Declaration of Human Rights, which set global standards not only for civil and political rights but for health, housing, and education. Asked to resign during the cold war, she was the target of McCarthyite attacks. "Once more," she said, "we are in a period of uncertainty, of danger, in which not only our own safety but that of all mankind is threatened. Once more we need the qualities that inspired the development of the democratic way of life. We need imagination and integrity, courage and a high heart." Her words resonate as much now as they did then.

GET PAST STATUS TO THE LEADER IN THE MIRROR

Fearless individualism — the quiet kind that doesn't need to be announced from the rooftops — is another requirement for leadership. When we are fearlessly who we are, we don't need external validation, just an opportunity to express ourselves, live fully, and serve the world. Too often we confuse speaking out with alpha status — the lead actor taking the main stage. But sometimes we can speak out clearly without power or position. This is a true alternate model of leadership, the kind that depends not on external power but on internal strength.

Notions of status and hierarchy — and how to negotiate them — have been plaguing humans since we first appeared on the planet. I can't say for sure, but it wouldn't surprise me if Adam used that whole apple-eating incident as a weapon against Eve to claim superior status and decision-making power in their new digs.

We're social creatures, and trying to determine our place in the social hierarchy is a natural human instinct. The question is, how much of the determination of our own status do we outsource to others? And what is the connection between what we perceive our status to be and our own happiness?

Status has long been connected with wealth and acquisition. Implicit in this game of showing those "below" us that we're better because we've got more than they do is an acceptance that those "above" us are better because they, in turn, have more than we do. So there is fear in those below us and fear toward those above us.

No one really wins in this game. But the good news is that

playing it is entirely optional. Status based on hierarchy exists only to the extent that we choose to buy into it. My mother never did. She chose to opt out and instead took control of her own status and defined her own worth. So she was freed from the petty turf wars and ugly envy of the status game, freed from fear about how "they" ranked her and what privileges "they" would bestow on her. By deciding her own worth and radiating the confidence that comes with this, she was secure in her status regardless of her life's circumstances. Getting rid of the fear that the status game generated allowed my mother to connect in a much deeper way with people at all levels of life.

She cut through hierarchies and showed everyone fortunate enough to come into contact with her that we're all cut from the same cloth. She approached life by liking everybody, and because this feeling of trust and connection is contagious, everybody liked her right back.

One night, while I was living in London, a member of Parliament I was dating at the time brought Prime Minister Edward Heath to dinner. My mother was in the kitchen, where she could be found most of the time, talking to the plumber, who had come to fix a last-minute problem. As I was leaving the kitchen, I overheard my mother asking the plumber what he thought of the prime minister. I didn't hear his reply, but a few minutes later my mother had engineered a sit-down between the prime minister and the plumber around the kitchen table so they could talk things out.

Later in life she put into practice her beliefs that there is no job that is beneath anybody and that one's status is not determined by what one does for a living but by the qualities and dignity one brings to the job. In the midseventies, she went to Los Angeles for an extended visit with my sister, Agapi, and her then husband. After about a month, when it became clear that my sister's husband would rather not live with his mother-in-law, my mother, not wanting to bother anybody, decided she would just strike out on her own.

But to do this, she was going to need a job. So she thought about what she knew how to do, what her talents were. What she came up with was that she knew how to manage a home — cooking, cleaning, and making everything run smoothly, on time, and with a minimum of friction. It was what she'd done all her life, and she was good at it. She put an ad in the paper looking for someone who needed a house manager. Lo and behold, she got a call back, went for the interview, and got the job. So she found herself in Santa Barbara, taking care of a beautiful family and their teenage kids, all of whom immediately fell in love with her. Aside from all the household duties, my mother would counsel the whole family on her organizational ideas, which she dubbed "creative order." More often than not, the kids would end up in my mother's room, talking through their problems with her.

She had taken the job with no sense of inferiority, and so it never occurred to the family to treat her as inferior. She simply went there to be of service and to earn a living, never forgetting exactly who she was. And, of course, when she got her first paycheck, she tried to give it to Agapi and me because she said she didn't need money, since she already had room and board.

Her adventure ended when I called her and asked her to please come to London. I need you, I told her, if I'm ever going to finish this book. My mother had never been able to resist a call of need from one of her daughters. So she flew to London and managed my little flat instead, keeping the kitchen going all night while I was furiously working to meet my self-imposed deadline.

Her job in Santa Barbara had been one more way that she taught her daughters by example how to cut through hierarchies and never wait for authority and leadership to be granted from without. Her solutions to problems would sometimes seem simple and obvious, but that was because of the fearlessness and trust with which she approached the world and moved through it.

So while we continue our efforts to open doors and break through glass ceilings, there is a lot we can do in the meantime, without permission from any person or institution, simply by connecting with the leader in the mirror.

Marie Wilson, an advocate of women's rights for more than thirty years, is the founder of the White House Project, an organization that promotes women's leadership in all spheres, including the presidency. As she herself admits, she hasn't lacked for fear — or resistance — along the way. "I have been afraid almost constantly," she told me. "I feared moving to New York from Iowa, where I raised my family, but I took the job as president of the Ms. Foundation for Women in the early eighties. I found myself demeaned by very important people when I championed microenterprise for low-income women in the eighties (they said it would marginalize the women it was meant to help), but now it is an accepted strategy worldwide. When I cocreated Take Our Daughters (and now Sons) to Work Day, I was told by a major donor at Ms. that it was the craziest idea I'd ever had. Now the day is almost a national holiday and it has helped millions of girls and adults.

"Of course, it's simple to look back and tell myself how brave I was in the face of intractable opposition to my ideas. Truthfully, there were nights that I shook till dawn and days when I cried till dusk. It takes a certain amount of hubris to go forward, not to dive for the covers when you are humiliated in public, to hold your vision when everyone else thinks you're crackers. Luckily, I'm just a little bit nuts that way."

It's not necessary to move to New York or Washington to lead. What all of us can do is begin to exercise leadership in our most immediate circles: our families and our communities. Because change doesn't happen just from the top down, and because leadership is increasingly rare at the top.

FEARLESS AT ANY COST

One of the hardest — and potentially most fear-inducing — aspects of speaking out is upsetting friends who might disagree with your opinions. Some of your friends might even become former friends as a result. You can only imagine how true this was for me when, in 1995, I started publicly criticizing some of my Republican friends in my syndicated column, and how much more intense it all became after I left the Republican Party at the end of 1996. I'll never forget a dinner party in 1996 at the Washington home of Boyden Gray, White House counsel to the first President Bush and a Beltway fixture. The guest list was a conservative Who's Who, with Mr. and Mrs. Rush Limbaugh as the guests of honor. "Why is she here?" Mrs. Limbaugh asked our host as I walked in. You see, I had dared question Limbaugh's compassion in a column. "Is the conservative movement going to be defined by the social Darwinism and carping small-mindedness of Limbaugh, or by the generous civic-mindedness that was central to America's founding?" I had asked. Rush's now-former bride was angry that I would be allowed to breathe the same air, eat the same food, and drink the same wine as her saintly husband. When I was informed of Mrs. Limbaugh's rage, I decided simply to make sure we were not within dinner roll–throwing distance of each other (about twenty-five feet, I estimated).

The evening had just begun, and the dining room was already looking like trouble: a buffet of beefs, gripes, and grudges, barely under wraps and sure to be revealed as the evening continued. While keeping one eye on the Limbaughs and the other on the exits, I tried to mingle.

In one corner I spotted Dick Armey, then Republican House majority leader, and his wife, Susan. Susan had a clothing store in Virginia at the time, and my daughters and I would occasionally stop in on a Saturday. Susan would help my girls, then five and three, play dress-up, allowing their mother to, well, also play dress-up. Her warmth and humor, coupled with the fact that she and I are both five foot ten and like the same midcalf skirts and long jackets, made me really like her.

So there I was, face-to-face with the Armeys for the first time since writing in a column that the House majority leader's "ersatz, insipid, and duplicitous style is only bringing him contempt." I had ended the column by saying that "the increasingly inescapable conclusion is that Gingrich and Armey, his presumptive heir apparent, need to go together." I didn't say where, exactly, but it was clear I didn't mean Disneyland.

The repercussions of the opinions I had been expressing twice weekly in my column — as well as on radio and TV and in speeches around the country — were now bouncing all over the room. "What has happened to Arianna?" my conservative friends were asking. It was scary to realize that my friendships were being seriously affected. As to what had happened to me, it can be summed up by one particular moment. That moment was on January 24, 1993. I was giving a speech at a Conservative Summit in Washington organized by the *National Review.* My speech was entitled "Can Conservatives Have a Social Conscience?" I was preceded by conservative media critic Brent Bozell, who gave a bullying speech of hard-right homilies. He got a standing ovation.

Fear began to rise in me — the special fear that comes when you suspect you're about to address a hostile audience. I approached the podium with trepidation, wondering what an audience that had applauded the previous speaker's harsh brand of conservatism would do with mine, which challenged all of us to rise to what I considered the core of true conservatism: the biblical admonition that we shall be judged by what we do for the least among us.

"Mrs. Huffington's goal is the redemption of the Republican Party," Karen DeWitt wrote in an article on the event in the *New York Times:* "If she had her way, greed and selfishness will be banished forever, to be replaced by altruism, compassion, and the 'kinder, gentler' world that George Bush talked about but failed to deliver." She went on to express the opinion that "it is an odd notion to link altruism and compassion with conservatives, considering last year's Republican convention."

But I never considered compassion and concern for social justice the exclusive province of Democrats, and I truly believed at the time that it wasn't too late to challenge the Republican Party to hark back to the noble traditions of its past. Apparently neither did the crowd, because they gave me a standing ovation, too. I realized that day that the problem was not with rank-and-file Republicans but with the party's leaders.

My conclusion was that I had simply appealed to different parts of their brains and their psyches than Bozell — to a component of social conscience without which individual responsibility is reduced to nothing but self-interest.

But, as I hardly need to tell you, the party leaders didn't exactly agree with me, and the social challenge I issued that morning was never taken up. The hope and expectation that people would roll up their sleeves and get their hands dirty to solve social problems at the local level was never realized. There were never enough volunteers, never enough donations, never enough model partnerships and pilot projects to prove what we conservatives claimed: that we could solve America's ills without "big government."

So at the heart of my political transformation was my recognition that the task of overcoming poverty and social injustice is too monumental to be achieved without the power and scale that only government can provide. Along with this came the conviction that silence is not an option. And we cannot let friendships stop us from speaking out about what we believe are fundamental truths.

Back in Boyden Gray's living room, I was experiencing how this decision played out on the personal level. Dick Armey, ever the politician, simply exchanged pleasantries with me, ignoring the fact that I had publicly wished him out of a job. But Susan fearlessly spoke her mind. "Arianna," she said, "how could you do that? How could you say those things about Dick? You were our friend." I mumbled some stock phrases about how it wasn't personal, just a reflection of our different political views, but Susan was hurt rather than angry, which is always much harder to deal with.

Thankfully, that squirm-inducing moment was interrupted by our host urging us on to dinner. Four round tables with calligraphed place cards awaited us. I found my seat between Senator Bill Frist and columnist (now White House press secretary) Tony Snow. I was already deep in conversation with the senator about the Washington school our kids attended when I noticed that Susan had just taken her seat across from me. The Limbaughs, mercifully, were seated at a different table, but I remained very aware of my unfinished conversation with Susan. When I saw her get up from the table, I followed her. We stood in the hallway for twenty minutes, talking — me trying to explain why it's no use even trying to write about politics if you censor yourself when it comes to your friends, Susan insisting that loyalty to one's friends is a higher principle than politics and that if you can't say something nice . . .

We were completely engaged in our conversation, having missed dessert, when Dick, who despite his flaws as a politician (I'd rather not get started on that) has flawless social graces, came to find out what was going on. We're fine, we both said. After he left, we hugged each other. If we couldn't be allies, at least we could strike up a détente.

Loyalty to one's friends is an important principle. But so is fearlessly speaking and writing about what you believe in — otherwise, why bother to speak or write at all?

My problems with personal acquaintances or friends being upset over my publicly expressed views did not end after the shift in my political views had stopped being a novelty. I have, after all, often been critical of new friends and new allies, people I inevitably run into on social occasions. Like weddings. A few years ago, I was attending one in Washington in which the best man was campaign consultant Bob Shrum. "Oh, no," I thought as I saw him walk down the aisle. I'd just written a column slamming him for his work on Al Checchi's failed bid for governor of California — a particularly fetid example of the nasty, small-minded campaigns that have befouled our political air. The vicious ads he ran had the effect of making Checchi, who began the campaign looking like Tony Perkins at the start of *Psycho,* look like Perkins at the end of *Psycho.*

At the lunch following the wedding, Shrum, looking very elegant — a morning coat and tails can have that effect — had trouble mustering a smile. It was a clear departure from the past. He and I had locked horns on many occasions on *Crossfire,* but it was always clear that we liked each other. I had known his wife even before they were married, and he had even been exceptionally nice helping me with my carry-on luggage and my carry-on seven-year-old on a red-eye flight to Washington. (What more could a woman ask for?)

At one point during the lunch, our paths crossed. "If I had

wanted to be critical about you," he said, "I would have called you and told you on the phone instead of putting it in a column."

But what I had written was not a personal criticism but a passionate denunciation of consultants and pollsters hijacking the political process and reducing everything to the lowest possible sound-bite-able denominator. It's often not pretty, but it's a lousy idea for us to hold our tongue in the public forum for fear it will upset someone we know.

After John Kerry lost the 2004 presidential election, I wrote a column assessing blame, and some of it fell squarely in the lap of, yes . . . Bob Shrum. By then I had also become friends with his stepson Michael Palmer, who was an occasional hiking partner and procurer of the best mix CDs on the west side of Los Angeles. "Are you still talking to me?" I asked Michael when I ran into him at a party a few months after I had blasted his stepfather in print. "I probably wouldn't have been right after you wrote your column," he replied, "but I am now." I breathed a deep sigh of relief. At least my supply of mix CDs was safe.

The consequences of speaking out fearlessly cut even closer to home when my daughter Isabella's godmother, who happened to be Elaine Chao, married Senator Mitch McConnell, whom I had often castigated for having been — among other things — one of the biggest obstacles to campaign finance reform. As if this were not enough, George Bush went ahead and nominated Elaine to be secretary of labor. And her nomination was confirmed. So there she was, part of an administration that I kept insulting on practically a daily basis. She was gracious enough to give Isabella a tour of the Labor Department when we were in Washington for spring break a few years ago, but it was clear that Isabella needed a godmother whose relationship with her goddaughter was not encumbered by her mother's political views. So I asked Isabella to pick a new godmother among my girlfriends.

All's well that ends well. After all, how many girls get to pick their own godmother? Isabella ended up choosing my friend Lynda Resnick. Among all the other good things in their relationship, Lynda owns POM Wonderful juice, which allows her to keep her goddaughter supplied with pomegranates (Isabella's favorite food) all year round.

Whatever the personal price, we must speak out about what matters. The world needs the leadership of women now more than ever. We may lose friends in the process, but we can no longer afford to remain silent.

Jody Williams on fearlessness

I AM PRIVILEGED to work with many women who are viewed by people around the world as being fearless, including my Nobel Peace Prize laureate sisters Shirin Ebadi, Rigoberta Menchu Tum, Wangari Mathai, and especially Aung San Suu Kyi, who struggles for democracy for her people by the sheer force of her personality even as she continues to be locked away under house arrest by the brutal military dictatorship in Burma.

While each of these women gives off an aura of fearlessness, even in the face of armed conflict, I do not believe that there is any one of us who is immune to fear. It is the choices we make in confronting it that shape who we are.

As a child, I was quiet, introverted, and anxious. Afraid of authority, I was particularly fearful about being yelled at and avoided all confrontation.

My own journey of wrestling my fears to the ground probably began with my older brother, Stephen, who had been born deaf. As is often the case with kids, other boys in the neighborhood were cruel to him. Their taunts made me sick and angry, and I began to try to defend him.

At first I would break out in a cold sweat and my insides would churn, but gradually it became natural to side with those being treated unfairly and unable to speak for themselves.

Growing up, I began to realize that many opinions people form about others have more to do with themselves than with the other person. It really didn't seem to matter what one did or did not do. Others would filter everything through their own views and come up with their own version of events anyway.

I came to believe that the only person's opinion that matters is your own. You have to be true to yourself and not stray from that, and find the courage to live as you see fit. I can still be anxious and fearful of things unknown. But I'm not afraid to do what I believe is right to confront inequalities and injustice in the world, and to try to make it a better place.

And as I reflect on the women I mentioned at the beginning, this seems a common thread in their lives as well. They might not always be comfortable or happy or free of worry for the future, but they are firm in their beliefs, they are not swayed, they are true to themselves. For all of us, it seems to be the only way to live a just life.

Nobel Prize winner Jody Williams founded the International Campaign to Ban Landmines.

$\mathcal{F}$earless About Changing the World

Conquer Your Fears and Make a World of Difference

NOW WE GET to the question: Beside the obvious increase in the quality of one's own life that comes from not being plagued by fear, what else can we do with this newfound courage?

Here's my suggestion: Change the world.

Sure, we're aiming high. But why not? Shouldn't the question of what to do with fearlessness be answered in a fearless way?

CHANGE OURSELVES, CHANGE THE WORLD

"If you wanted to put the world to rights," asked Alexander Solzhenitsyn, who spent years imprisoned in the Soviet gulag for trying to change *his* world, "who should you begin with: yourself or others?"

Before he died in 1995, Jonas Salk devoted most of his time to speaking and writing about changing the world by changing ourselves. "If we look at evolution as an error-making and an error-correcting process, and if we are ever so much slightly better at error-correcting than at error-making, we'll make it." When I visited Salk at his home in La Jolla in the mideighties, he spoke of evolution in spiritual terms. "The evolutionary instinct compels us to bring out the best in ourselves and in others, to recognize our interconnectedness with everyone else," he told me. He was referring not to the first instinct, survival, but to the fourth that drives us "to bring out the best."

Man, created in God's image, has free will. We have exercised free will to pick our mates and plague our enemies, to forge our steel and launch our rockets. And we can apply this same will to our evolution. We will evolve whether we choose to or not, but suppose we decided to seek every opportunity to fearlessly evolve to be the best we can be? What then? How much easier would it be to change the world?

Of course, if your goal is changing the world, fear is not an unreasonable response, especially for an "uppity woman" (a.k.a. any woman who expresses an opinion that doesn't simply confirm traditional ideas and the status quo). She can reliably expect to get a lot of grief for stepping out of her prescribed roles. But if the choice is between being considered "uppity" for not going along and going along simply to get along, I'll take the former. And if you've made it this far in the book, I suspect and hope you will, too.

THE PRICE OF ACTIVISM

It doesn't matter what world you're in — business, journalism, fashion, politics, your church, or your family — the status quo doesn't like having its cage rattled. Especially by a woman.

As Tom DeLay put it in referring to Hillary Clinton, there's "nothing worse than a woman know-it-all." I, in fact, have exactly the opposite problem with Hillary. She's too afraid she's going to offend some group of likely voters if she stops playing the "all things to all people" card and starts really leading. (And what does soft-pedaling her views get her? She gets criticized for coming on strong anyway, even when she doesn't.)

You don't have to be a famous politician to draw attacks. Lois Gibbs, head of the Center for Health, Environment and Justice in Washington, DC, used to be a working-class housewife. In 1978, she was attacked for having the gall to organize her neighbors in Love Canal, New York, to fight a toxic dump that resulted in fifty-six children in the area born with extra teeth, fingers, or ears, and mental retardation.

When the government wouldn't conduct the necessary safety studies, Gibbs's group stepped in. "The New York State health department," Gibbs said, "literally threw our report on the floor and said it was useless housewife data, collected by women who have a vested interest in the outcome."

For daring to care about her community and speak up, Gibbs got the treatment reserved for "uppity" women. "The government people would say things to me like, 'Well, Mrs. Gibbs, if your children are so sick, why aren't you home taking care of them?' They would try to belittle me, right down to correcting me publicly if I mispronounced something."

This response is certainly not new. It's just a continuation of the hostility faced through the years by women who've wanted to change the world.

Indifference was the best one could hope for. When Elizabeth Cady Stanton presented the Women's Suffrage Amendment to Congress in 1878, the men in Congress simply ignored her. "The particularly aggravating feature," Stanton wrote, "was the studied inattention and contempt of the chairman, Sen. Wadleigh of New Hampshire, who alternately looked over manuscripts and newspapers, jumped up and down to open or close a door or a window, stretched, yawned, gazed at the ceiling, cut his nails, sharpened his pencil."

Alice Paul, a leader of the National Women's Party, had to deal with a lot worse than indifference. She was jailed in a psychiatric prison for her protests in 1917 (which included demonstrating during President Woodrow Wilson's speeches) and force-fed after she began leading a hunger strike.

Throughout history, tens of thousands of women have been tried as witches and hanged or burned at the stake. "There were moments," Arthur Miller writes about the Salem witch trials in *The Crucible,* "when an individual conscience was all that could keep the world from falling apart." Carol Karlsen at the University of Michigan studied hundreds of cases of accused witches and of a world falling apart in colonial New England. In her book *The Devil in the Shape of a Woman,* she writes that grounds for the charge of witchcraft included being "aggressive and abrasive . . . ill tempered, quarrelsome, and spiteful," behaviors considered evil, and threatening the power hierarchy and the will of God.

Most of these women, according to Karlsen, were over forty and tended to be single, widowed, or divorced (i.e., manless). Sometimes they had had premarital sex, sometimes they were bold enough to petition in court for inheritance or other rights, sometimes they were simply the scapegoat after a bad crop season or the death of someone beloved in the community. "The witch image," she writes, "sets off in stark relief the most cherished values of these societies."

We no longer declare "uppity" women witches, we just dub them "hysterical" or dismiss them as irrational and overemotional when they make demands that society finds annoying, challenging, or threatening.

In the twentieth century, treatment for "hysterical" women included electroshock therapy and medication. Lots of medication. "Shock treatment," Peter Breggin, author of *Toxic Psychiatry*, writes, "has been used to erase the memories and even the personalities of patients, usually women." He recounts how one therapist, H. C. Tien, used shock therapy in the 1970s on women "to 'reprogram' them as more suitable wives with their husbands' help." Not exactly the robotic spousal transformation of *The Stepford Wives*, but pretty damn close.

If you don't want to go all high-tech with your "uppity" reprogramming, you can get the same results with a little pill. In 1963, the tranquilizer Valium was introduced and prescribed to millions of housewives. It became the most prescribed drug in America from 1969 until 1982. Think *Desperately Sedated Housewives*.

IN PRAISE OF "HYSTERICAL" WOMEN

At every period in history, there has been a price to pay for being an agent of change. But there is also a price to pay for living timidly — and a lot less upside. Squashing our true selves is a major cause of fear, anxiety, and depression. According to the National Alliance on Mental Illness, women experience clinical depression two to three times as much as men. Our culture's solution is more drugs. Billions of advertising dollars are spent convincing consumers that personal suffering can be eradicated through drugs — a pill for every ill.

There are, of course, chemical imbalances that require medication, but something is definitely off-kilter when we medicate and silence ourselves instead of changing what is not working in our lives — and in our world.

THE REWARDS OF RISK

The impulse to follow the voice not of fear but of our fourth instinct and fight to make the world a better place is as present in our DNA as the drive to improve our own lives. That's why fearlessness — refusing to be controlled by threats, guilt, blame, even praise and blandishments — is more than indispensable; it's our true calling as human beings.

The rewards of great courage, of being a pioneer, are proportionate to the risks we take. If not for Alice Paul and the women's suffrage movement, women might still not have the right to vote. If not for Lois Gibbs, hundreds of families might not have been relocated to healthier communities in the 1970s and thousands of others would not now have the center she founded to assist in cleaning up their own communities. There are few things as empowering as being in the presence of women who risk everything to change the world.

Naomi Wolf, author of *The Beauty Myth,* discovered this truth when she started to travel in the developing world. She encountered women who had lived through rape, slavery, mutilations, and other atrocities, and had stood up to oppression and injustice. "To young women in our culture," she told me, "approval is like oxygen — we are afraid that without it we will perish. But when I returned to New York after meeting these amazing women, the scale of my own fears seemed very small. Our ego-based fears — being derided or criticized or devalued — suddenly seemed very trivial. If it's not going to send me to a gulag or get me tortured, I now feel that, on behalf of other women who face real terror every day, I had best simply get on with it."

Every year since 1997, I have been exposed to fearless women leaders in the field of journalism. They are the women from around the world who have won the International Women's Media Foundation's Courage in Journalism Award. They have risked their lives to report the truth about corruption and oppression in some of the world's most dangerous hot spots. No one handed them their power, no one elected them, no one expected them to act as leaders. But each in her own way broke from the pack, compelled to seek out the truth and tell it. And each in her own way has changed our world.

One of these fearless women to whom I presented the award in Los Angeles in 1997 is Bina Bektiati from Indonesia. Soft-spoken and reticent, she was probably the last person the Indonesian government expected to resist when it shut down *Tempo*, the newspaper she worked for, in 1994. But she refused to work for the government paper that replaced *Tempo* and went on to protest by helping to create the Alliance of Independent Journalists. After the government banned all members of the alliance from writing, Bektiati started using a pseudonym.

But she considers "internalized censorship" even more chilling than the censorship imposed by the Indonesian government. "They have succeeded in transforming censorship into self-censorship," she lamented in her acceptance speech. "We don't need warning telephone calls anymore, and the army doesn't have to threaten anyone. We have become 'good' journalists by censoring ourselves, and that is what our government calls a 'free and responsible press.' Today, self-censorship is our worst nightmare."

As I listened to Bektiati speak, I was thinking of the self-censorship here in the freest country in the world. What have we internalized? What have we accepted as normal? What are the boundaries of our curiosity? What things, either through myopia or mental flabbiness, do we no longer hear or see? What are our self-imposed limits? What would the consequences be if we simply decided to step over these limits?

Maribel Gutiérrez was another fearless woman being honored that day. In her home of Guerrero, Mexico, the poorest of the country's thirty-two states, it takes enormous courage to challenge the neglect of struggling communities. Which is what she's been doing as one of the founders of *El Sur*, a newspaper that has fearlessly exposed corruption and human-rights violations. And for that, her name was put on a blacklist disseminated by government agents.

The final honoree was Corinne Dufka, an American who left the safety of her native country to document the anguish in the world's killing fields. She was born in Connecticut and raised in northern Utah, but her life as a Reuters photojournalist in El Salvador, Rwanda, Burundi, Somalia, Ethiopia, Sudan, and Bosnia could not be farther from the world of her upbringing. She wants, as she put it, "to portray in images both the grief and human suffering brought on by war, as well as the human strength involved in people simply trying to live their lives and love their families within the devastating context of war." Four of her friends at Reuters were killed — not in combat but for the images they brought to light.

In a culture obsessed with trivial fears, trifling vanities, and social anxieties, being exposed to the lives of women like Bina, Maribel, and Corinne is invigorating, a wake-up call that shakes us out of our torpor. We nudge up against another reality and are reminded of the wide range of possibilities available to us. Which is why all of us leaving that hotel ballroom were a little different — a little less fearful — than we had been walking in.

THE MUCH BIGGER PICTURE

Even if the stakes do not involve standing up to oppression and corruption and improving the lives of millions, it's much easier to go fearlessly on your own life's journey when the destination you've chosen includes something larger than yourself.

In a study on the roots of altruism, Dr. Ervin Staub analyzed men and women who had risked their lives during World War II to protect Jews hiding from the Nazis. What turns an ordinary bystander into a fearless defender? "Goodness, like evil, often begins in small steps," Dr. Staub says. "Heroes evolve: They aren't born. Very often the rescuers made only a small commitment at the start — to hide someone for a day or two — but once they had taken that step they began to see themselves differently, as someone who helps. What starts as mere willingness becomes intense involvement."

Indeed, heroes evolve, but heroism wouldn't blossom if the seed for fearlessness, for goodness, for transcending our self-interest had not been planted a *long* time ago. This potential to move beyond our daily concerns and personal ambitions is our common heritage, a seed waiting to be watered by a few drops of courage and compassion.

As Anna Quindlen said in her Women's Commission for Refugee Women and Children speech: "With great gains we must always be careful of our potential losses, and if we become the sort of people who believe, as a group, that the position of our name on the page or the letterhead is the most important thing about you, we will, as the Bible verse goes, have gained the whole world and lost our immortal souls. . . . The point was never the corner office. The point was sisterhood, solidarity, freedom, and, above all, peace. The point of the whole thing was the whole wide world."

Oprah Winfrey echoes Quindlen's conclusion: "The real beauty of having material wealth is that you don't have to worry about paying the bills and you have more energy to be concerned about the things that matter. How do I accelerate my humanity? How do I use who I am on earth for a purpose that's bigger than myself?"

This is the common theme in the lives of fearless women: Fear is much easier to overcome when the focus of our lives moves beyond ourselves to a cause we are passionate about.

Dorothy Day, a journalist, a single mother, and Catholic convert born at the end of the nineteenth century, started the *Catholic Worker* — a newspaper dedicated to giving voice to those impoverished by the Depression — from her kitchen table. The paper's message of service and charity led to the founding of the first "hospitality house" offering food, clothing, and shelter to anyone who needed them. (There are now more than 185 in operation.) Day's muckraking articles and social activism flowed directly out of her fearless spirit and religious faith. And she was willing to pay the price for her dedication, which included sometimes alienating her own comrades and even repeated arrests. But after her death, her relentless devotion to social justice led to a movement to canonize her. "Don't call me a saint," she famously scoffed. "I don't want to be dismissed so easily."

Rory Kennedy, who admits that she is sometimes unnerved by even ordinary things like escalators and ski lifts, also found that the wider the focus of her life, the more her fears were dissolved. So even in the most anxious situations, she found herself emboldened: "I did a film about the global AIDS crisis, and in the process went into clinics where people are dying of AIDS. So much death and suffering are always hard to confront, but I really try not to avoid them, and it definitely puts my own fears in perspective. For example, it's hard for me to speak in public, but I make myself do it because I'm talking about people whose voices are rarely heard, and I feel I have the opportunity to give them a platform. So whatever fears and reservations I have, I can put them aside because there is something more important. Often when I do speaking engagements, just before I go on stage I think of Leck, who died of AIDS. I think about her and remind myself of why I'm doing what I'm doing, and it helps me put aside all the questions going on in my head and come from my heart instead."

FULFILLMENT THROUGH FEARLESSNESS, AND VICE VERSA

There is a correlation not only between helping others and fearlessness but, as scientists have shown, between any kind of charitable behavior and improved health, improved immune function, and improved ability to cope with illness and disability. Healing ourselves, making ourselves whole by helping others, is not some half-baked homily. As psychiatrist Karl Menninger has observed, "Love cures people. Both the ones who give it, and the ones who receive it." Those who make giving a big part of their lives discover that it's actually the highest form of selfishness.

Susan Kaiser Greenland was successful in her hectic twenty-year career in entertainment law and happy in her marriage to writer Seth Greenland, with two great kids. But there was something missing. "My children were in search of almost constant stimulation," she told me. "They were not experiencing something that had existed in the slower pace of my childhood. I decided to try to adapt for them the mindfulness and meditation practices that had helped me. I started by teaching them to our younger child. He used his breath to slow down when he was overexcited and to calm down when he was upset. Something seemed to be working and I thought I could take it out into the world."

Susan started small, volunteering a couple of hours a week in the after-school day care at the local Boys and Girls Club. In 2001, she and Seth founded the not-for-profit InnerKids, through which she's taught hundreds of classes in both public and private settings from prekindergarten through middle school. "When I saw the hunger that existed for this," she says, "I realized that my days as a full-time lawyer were over, and I closed my law firm."

Bonnie Paul facilitates a workshop, sponsored by the University of Santa Monica, on forgiveness among women in prison. She reached out to a forgotten, often despised segment of the population and in the process was able to overcome her own fears of the unknown, of public speaking, and of the very people she wanted to help.

"Valley State Prison for Women," she told me, "is a medium-to-maximum-security prison, and our first workshop was attended by women serving ten-year-to-life sentences. I completely subscribed in concept to the idea that all people are equally worthy of love and respect. But I'd never had the courage to put myself in a situation where that ideal would be tested. And I was terrified. In the weeks of preparations before the first workshop I would wake up remembering dreams full of fearful images: getting trapped in the prison, prison riots, and violence. Hearing from our prison staff contact about repeated bomb threats at the prison didn't help. Added to these fears was my severe fear of public speaking. It was so bad that my throat would close up and my voice would come out like a croak. When the first day came, my level of fear was nearly crippling. 'Please God, help me!' I would repeat inwardly each time I got up to speak. Finally I decided to share my fear with the inmates. It was a risk, but the fear's power over me was dramatically diminished as soon as I had acknowledged it. Also, sharing my fear helped the inmates connect with me."

Bonnie just completed her fifth workshop. A number of the women have taken the workshop four and five times, and they serve as inspiration for their peers, teaching what they have learned to women who are preparing to return to society. But what also strikes Bonnie is the change in herself: less fear and greater inner strength as a result of the changes she helped bring about in others. As the Reverend Henry Delaney, who has been transforming boarded-up crack houses in Savannah, Georgia, once told me: "I want to get people involved. It's like putting a poker in the fire. After a while, the fire gets in the poker, too."

PLAYING POLITICS

If you're going to try to change the world through politics, it's all the more important to bring some of the qualities of fearlessness so desperately needed at a time when politicians are often paralyzed by the fear that they will offend some group of likely voters.

Recently elected German chancellor Angela Merkel is displaying some of this fearlessness. The first woman (and first East German) to hold the post, she took a stand early on when she refused to spy for the secret police as a teen. A PhD in physics, she was selected by former chancellor Helmut Kohl as minister for women and youth. Leapfrogging over others in her male-dominated party, she now manages the balancing act of leading a "grand coalition" government. The woman Kohl once nicknamed *"das Mädchen"* (the girl) told a German women's magazine during her campaign, "Never before in my political life have I been taken so seriously as a woman as in the past few months."

Here in the United States, Assemblywoman Karen Bass, who now represents California's Forty-seventh District, was a physician's assistant in the largest emergency trauma center in the country, where she saw the toll drugs and poverty were taking on her community. This led her to found the Community Coalition, to address violence, voting, health care, and other local concerns. For Karen, running for office was not only the next step in serving her community but a way to diversify local government.

"I ran against four men," she told me, "which was a real challenge. I felt like I was running against the old-boys' club. And there hadn't been an African American woman in the state legislature in years."

Being elected, of course, is not the only way to get involved in politics. Legal action is another way. Lynn Schenk was one of only four women in her 1970 law school graduating class at a time when some judges wouldn't even acknowledge women lawyers and many law firms wouldn't hire them. The career she forged as an attorney in California state and federal governments might never have been possible if she and other women hadn't banded together to create new opportunities and challenge gender-biased laws. "We formed the Lawyers' Club, which today is one thousand strong," she told me, "and the Women's Bank so that women could get credit in their own names."

And they went to court and to the legislature. "We changed the community property laws, we changed the credit laws, we changed every discriminatory law we could find on the books."

When the fearlessness we need in the world of politics is exemplified by women, it is, of course, likely to be met with hostility, called "out of control," or simply dismissed. When Ségolène Royal announced she might run for the presidency of France, a former prime minister (and political rival) asked, "Who's going to look after the children?" And a senator snarked, "The presidential race is not a beauty contest."

I got a taste of this attitude firsthand when I ran for governor of California. But the biggest lesson I took away from that experience is that being "in the ring," fighting the good fight, whether through running for office or speaking or writing or organizing, is always more fulfilling, more exhilarating, and more effective than watching the battle from the sidelines. You may not win the contest, but that doesn't mean you don't win.

ON BECOMING FEARLESS ABOUT CHANGING THE WORLD

All right, good for them, you say, but what can *I* do? The answer: more than you might ever imagine.

As William James writes, "The greatest revolution of our generation is the discovery that human beings, by changing the inner attitudes of their minds, can change the outer aspects of their lives." In other words, the first step toward changing the world is to change our vision of the world and of our place in it. After all, what we learn, both from our own lives and from the lives of public figures, is that character is not static. James Q. Wilson sums it up in *The Moral Sense:* "To say that people have a moral sense is not the same thing as saying that they are innately good. A moral sense must compete with other senses that are natural to humans — the desire to survive, acquire possessions, indulge in sex, or accumulate power — in short, with self-interest narrowly defined. How that struggle is resolved will differ depending on our character, our circumstances, and the cultural and political tendencies of the day. But saying that a moral sense exists is the same thing as saying that humans, by their nature, are potentially good."

We build up our moral muscle by exercising it. We become virtuous by the practice of virtue, responsible by the practice of responsibility, generous by the practice of generosity, and compassionate by the practice of compassion. So, the moment *we* begin to change, the world starts changing with us because we're all interconnected.

AN EPIDEMIC OF FEARLESSNESS

My optimism about our power to create social change comes from the possibilities embedded in the concept of "critical mass": When a change establishes itself in a few, it can quickly hit critical mass and spread to the many. To a physicist, critical mass is the amount of radioactive material that must be present for a nuclear reaction to become self-sustaining. In everyday life, critical mass is the phenomenon Malcolm Gladwell popularized in *The Tipping Point: How Little Things Can Make a Big Difference.* Ideas, behavior, messages, and products, he argues, often spread through the population like "outbreaks of infectious disease."

A single sick person can start a flu epidemic. So, too, can a few fare-beaters fuel a subway crime wave, or a handful of satisfied customers cause the empty tables of a new restaurant to fill. These are social epidemics, and the moment when they take off — when they reach their critical mass — is the tipping point. As Gladwell puts it, the tipping point is "the threshold, the boiling point. . . . It's the point on the graph where the line suddenly turns straight upward."

Reaching critical mass is just as important in the latest fashion trend as in major political, cultural, and social change. Any new way of being and of doing things manifests itself in the few before it spreads to the many. Social scientists have shown that a person's behavior frequently depends on the number of other people behaving in a given way. Whether it's an election, a protest, or a fund-raising drive for the local homeless shelter, this pattern can become self-sustaining and even accelerate once it passes a certain threshold of energy and involvement.

Wendy Kopp, who started Teach for America, believed that by placing a critical mass of top university graduates for two years as paid teachers in underserved rural and urban communities, we could, as she says, "build a movement to eliminate educational inequity. In the short run, the corps members have an impact as teachers in the lives of kids growing up today. In the long run, deeply influenced by their experience, they become a leadership force working for educational excellence and equity."

From the beginning, Kopp refused to think small, enlisting five hundred recruits. "I don't think Teach for America would exist today if we hadn't started out on that scale," she says. "It was critical to creating an aura of national importance and urgency."

And she raised funds in a fearless way: She just went out and asked top CEOs for the money and one of them actually made a seed grant. But in 1990, during the hectic first summer training session, all her fears came to the surface: "I withdrew into my shell. It got to the point where I even feared going to the cafeteria. And each night during our first year, I would wonder, 'Will the whole plan come crashing down?'"

What kept her moving forward, then as now, is her passion "to level the playing field for those students in underserved communities." Kopp believes that regardless of whether participants stay on as professional teachers or move into other careers, the Teach for America experience will cement their commitment to helping disadvantaged young people.

Once critical mass is reached and the change gains acceptance and becomes self-sustaining, those who started it will no longer be regarded as eccentric or uppity. They will be honored as pioneers. Mainstream recognition was bestowed on Wendy Kopp when she was invited by the president to sit next to Laura Bush in the gallery during the State of the Union address in 2002. The point of fearlessness is to follow the call of your soul, wherever it may lead, and ignite a spark that spurs others to do the same. It's what Dorothy Day called "a revolution of the heart."

CONNECT TO YOUR COMMUNITY

We begin to change the world when we rekindle our sense of community. The call to community is a call to belonging, to being a part of something larger than ourselves. And by connecting with others, we reconnect with the fearless part of ourselves.

Being raised in Athens, I was infused with that sense of community. The Golden Age of Greece was taught to me not as ancient history, as my children have learned it in school, but as my personal roots and source of identity. I knew myself as part of that timeless community. And in the home of my childhood, there was no division between community and spirituality, history and current events, even public issues and private concerns.

The call to community is not a hollow protestation of universal brotherhood. It is a call to make another's pain our own and to get in touch with our true fearless self through giving. This is not the cold abstraction of giving to humanity in general and to no human being in particular. It is concrete, intimate, tangible. And when the human spirit is awakened, there is no problem too intractable to solve.

MAKING SERVICE A FAMILY AFFAIR

It's never too late to get involved in volunteering. And it's never too soon to get our daughters, and our sons, to make it part of their lives. Isabel Kaplan is only sixteen years old, but she's already founded an organization, Girls for Girls, International, dedicated to helping young girls in developing countries gain access to education. "I ran into many roadblocks, money being one of the largest," she says. "But we kept overcoming them one at a time. If I had given in to the fear of failure, had backed down when something didn't work as I'd planned, I never would have had the opportunity to feel the joy that I felt when I printed Girls for Girls, International's first official brochure."

When volunteering becomes a family affair, overworked moms can serve their communities while spending quality time with their kids. Multitasking at its best! When I served on the board of the Points of Light Foundation in the 1990s, National Family Volunteer Day was an effort to bring together grass-roots organizations, corporate volunteer centers, and Fortune 100 companies with a single goal: getting children to join with their parents, grandparents, aunts, uncles, and siblings to make a difference in their communities.

The day isn't some feel-good act of noblesse oblige, a camera-ready photo op timed for the annual pre-Thanksgiving pity parade ("Oh, look, Bob — it's the always heart-tugging soup kitchen float, followed by the giant homeless guy balloon. The kids just love him!"). It's an answer to the pervasive narcissism of our consumption-crazy culture. And so are all the year-round efforts at family volunteering. Children brought up to feel that their lives have a larger purpose beyond themselves are more likely to keep their own troubles in perspective and less likely to fall into drugs or, at the extreme, open fire on their classmates.

America is plagued with disconnections — blacks from whites, rich from poor, and, perhaps most troubling, parents from children. One of the greatest ways to bridge these divides is by teaching children from an early age the importance of making service an integral part of their lives. It helps them to move beyond the fear of not being popular to the value of being useful.

My primary responsibility at the Points of Light Foundation was to work with those trying to make family volunteering an essential part of the American culture. The goal — and the hope — was that when families gathered around to decide what they were going to do on weekends — go to the mall? see a movie? hit the beach? — volunteering would be among the regular options.

For my own kids, volunteering together has been a profound educational experience; they've absorbed lessons they could easily have rejected if I had just preached them. I remember the first time I took them to a center for at-risk children in Anacostia called Children of Mine run by Hannah Hawkins, a remarkable and fearless woman. They were seven and five at the time, and we were living in Washington. My kids helped prepare the table for dinner and played with the children at the center. As it happened, it was one of the little girls' fifth birthday, and my daughter Isabella had just celebrated hers. As the little girl was blowing out the candle on the cupcake that was serving as both birthday cake and birthday present, I could see Isabella's eyes welling with tears. Without anyone saying anything to her, she made the comparison in her five-year-old mind between her birthday party, with all the presents and the balloons and the Little Mermaid cake, and this modest celebration she was now part of. When we got home, she gathered her birthday presents and told me that she wanted to give them to the little girls at Children of Mine.

Trust me, I know that overcoming selfishness and developing our muscles of giving and generosity are a lifetime's work. But exposing our daughters early on to the suffering in the world and to all the opportunities they have to do something about it is one of the greatest gifts we can give them — a gift that will help them transcend so many of the fears that are part of growing up in our narcissistic culture. And by planting these seeds early on, we'll help them make changing the world at least one item on their to-do list as they grow into fearless women.

Debrah Constance _on fearlessness_

I BEGAN LIFE as some kind of Grimms'-fairy-tale creature: large, undesirable, grossly imperfect. It got worse from there.

My father would tell me that he loved me as he abused me. After a few cocktails, he'd yell at me and slap me. Mother seldom did anything to protect me. My first husband, Tony, also started pounding on me. I would separate my mind from my body and just float around until it was over.

Then I met Dr. Raymond. Three days a week I would take my shattered Humpty Dumpty self to Dr. Raymond, who slowly helped me piece myself back together. I met a new man, got married, got pregnant with a much-wanted child. Six years later I had major surgery for cancer of the cervix and uterus. My ups and downs continued.

I started drinking at fourteen, so as not to feel. A total collapse at my sister's wedding led me to join Alcoholics Anonymous. After three years, I sponsored other women and saw their lives change one day at a time.

I started a career in real estate with Jon Douglas as head of community affairs. Working with students from Jefferson High, I met a girl who became my informal little sister. Meeting her family was my first personal experience of the profound poverty of South Central Los Angeles. Although I was earning $100,000 a year, I realized that I wanted to help children more than I wanted my salary.

I arranged to meet David Crippens, a consultant for nonprofits, who asked me, "What do you really want to do with your life?" No one had ever asked me that. I said, "All I want to do is open a safe house for the children from Jefferson High School, in South Central, where they can get off the street, have a snack, do their homework, and play." He said, "Write this down: 501c3. Look up information on raising money. You can do it."

When I told my boss that I was going to quit, he gave me six months' severance pay and an office. In a coffee shop later, a stranger offered to help me get my 501c3 tax exemption. And he did. He also helped me come up with the name: A Place Called Home.

The step-by-step tools I had learned in AA became a model for the work we do. I took the children who had drug, alcohol, and gang problems to AA meetings with me, then out to lunch. I loved it and so did they. We started Gangsters Anonymous, where hard-core gang members could speak honestly about their challenges.

But open conflict still reigned in the street. One day around Christmas, armed, snarling gang members — some of them as young as thirteen — materialized at the Bethel church near A Place Called Home. I walked right outside and said, "You put your guns down, or we're not going to celebrate Christmas, and you're not going to get any gifts." They did.

I saw how little it takes to distract children from habits of violence — a video, a music lesson, a basketball game, and the warrior transforms, right before your eyes, into an eager child.

I felt absolutely at ease with these children, because I could relate to the dangers they faced. I loved them without reservation.

In South Central, I have found *my* home. Everything that ever occurred in my life gave me the fearlessness to do what I do.

Debrah Constance is the founder of A Place Called Home, a center for at-risk youth in South Central Los Angeles.

Living the Fearless Life

WHEN WE KNOW who we are, we can overcome our fears and insecurities. We surpass our smaller selves who suffer the slings and arrows of our conditioned reality, and we move to the unconditional truth of our larger selves. The answers to the questions of what to say, what to do, whom to let in, and whom to keep out become a clear and simple matter of listening to our hearts. That inner voice helps us align with our purpose, because each of us has a purpose, even if we judge it to be insignificant. The voice is there. We just need to listen to it.

When we do that, we live in fearlessness.

Acknowledgments

———•·•———

This is undoubtedly the most personal book I've ever written. It springs from my life, my family, my relationships, and all my previous books. This is also the first book I've written since the creation of the Huffington Post — which was both a good thing and a bad thing. It was bad because, it turns out, writing a book while running a 24/7 Web site is not a match made in heaven (or even on Match.com). But it was good because I was able to post excerpts from the chapters I was working on, which produced immediate feedback and led to some great comments from readers about their own journeys from fear to fearlessness. (Sadly, many of these had to be cut after the first draft, when my editor told me I had to lose 20,000 words. In three days.)

Many thanks go to our L.A.-based Huffington Post team — Marja Adriance, Pete Keeley, Michael Owen, and Eric Stein — and Colin Sterling in our New York office for all their help with the book. And special thanks to our HuffPost editor, Roy Sekoff, for turning his LASIK-enhanced eagle eye on the final draft.

My gratitude goes to my remarkable editor, Tracy Behar, for all the ways in which she improved the manuscript while at the same time going to such great lengths to make sure it was completed in time, including flying cross-country to Los Angeles to finalize the editing by my side. Also many thanks to the rest of the Little, Brown team — Nneka Bennett, Sophie Cottrell, Caitlin Earley, Heather Fain, Peggy Freudenthal, Marie Mundaca, Mario Pulice, Heather Rizzo, Geoff Shandler, Mary Tondorf-Dick, Betsy Uhrig — and to publisher Michael Pietsch for all his support and insights.

Once again, for the fifth book running, I'm beyond grateful to my agent, Richard Pine, who, together with his good friend Liz Perle, came up with the subject for this book. Many thanks to Liz also for her superb editorial suggestions on the first draft.

Also to Miranda Spencer for being part of every stage of the book, from organizing the research to contributing her own story of fearlessness to reading the galleys.

Many thanks to Chris Kyle, Rachel Monroe, Ryan Watson, Lexi Vukcevicm, Brookes Nohlgren, and Elias Altman for all their help with research, fact-checking, and copyediting.

My gratitude to Stephen Sherrill, for reading and editing multiple versions of the manuscript, up to and including the one that came back from the copyeditor.

And many thanks to Patt Morrison, Romi Lassally, Lynn Sweet, and Shari Foos for reading what I thought was the final draft and then making so many good suggestions that another "I'm serious — this is the last one!" final draft quickly followed.

It's hard to imagine writing this book without my sister, Agapi

Stassinopoulos, who conducted many of the interviews for the book and provided me with many of its insights and a seemingly endless stream of memories about our childhoods, our mother, and many fearful and fearless stories from our lives.

To my daughters, Christina and Isabella, who are an inspiration for the book and who helped me write their stories in it, thank you for this, as well as for being the best thing in my life.

This book is built not just on my life and my personal experiences with both fear and fearlessness but also on the experiences of many generous women who shared their stories with me. Some appear in the book and some — Roseanne Barr, Suzanne Booth, Judith Cardamone, Alyce Faye Eichelberger, Judith Foster, Mary Golden, Audrey Greenberg, Gennifer Harding-Gosnell, Anna Kelner, Liz Lange, Maia Lazar, Sarah Magee, Mojgan Majdy, Melanie Maki, Rebecca L. Marks, S. P. Miskowski, Paul Muller, Julia Ormond, Natalie Smith Parra, Lise Paul, Laura Pedersen, Tiffany Persons, Debbie Phillips, Karen Powell, T. R. Sand, Jane Smiley, Brian Smith, Timothea Stewart, and Deborah Szekely — will appear in the portraits and stories of fearlessness we will run on the Huffington Post.

Finally, writing this book brought me closer to my mother and her fearless spirit than I've been since her death — adding to the immeasurable debt of gratitude I already owed her.

About the Author

Arianna Huffington was raised in Greece by her fearless mother and graduated from Cambridge University, where she headed its famed debating society. She has written eleven books, appeared on numerous television and radio shows, and founded the Huffington Post, an enormously successful online source of news and opinion. While taking on a variety of roles, Huffington has embodied the fearless woman throughout her life. In 2006 she was named by *Time* magazine one of the most influential people in the world. She has written this book for her two daughters in the hope that they will lead fearless lives.

ON BECOMING

FEARLESS

...in Love, Work, and Life

by Arianna Huffington

A Reading Group Guide

A CONVERSATION WITH THE AUTHOR OF
ON BECOMING FEARLESS

*Arianna Huffington talks with her daughters,
Christina and Isabella, about their fears—and about
the importance of spreading an epidemic of fearlessness.*

CHRISTINA: One of the things people ask me is, Isn't your mother afraid of anything? And I always say, Of course she is! Being fearless doesn't mean turning into Wonder Woman or some kind of superhero.

ARIANNA: Exactly. I always tell people that fearlessness is not the absence of fear, it's the mastery of fear. Fearlessness is about getting up one more time than we fall down—or are tripped by our critics!

One of the big messages I want women to take away from the book is that being fearless doesn't mean they are living a life devoid of fear but rather that they are living a life in which they don't allow their fears to hold them back and stop them from having what they want in their personal lives, in their work, and even in creating the world that we want to live in.

ISABELLA: But isn't that easier said than done?

ARIANNA: Well, fearlessness is like a muscle. I know from my own life that the more I exercise it the more natural it becomes to not let my fears run me. The first time we take that first fearless step, we begin to change our lives. And the more we act on our dreams and our desires, the more fearless we become and the easier it is the next time.

Being fearless has been the foundation of any success I have enjoyed—both personally and professionally. It's what's allowed me to persevere through the hard times—and as you know there have been plenty of those—and come out on the other side stronger and ready for the next challenge.

CHRISTINA: This is a different kind of book for you—less political, more personal. How did fearlessness play into the writing of it?

ARIANNA: It didn't make sense to write this kind of book without being willing to be vulnerable about my own battles with fear—and with some of the issues we've dealt with as a family. The personal aspect is part of what most appealed to me.

One of the things I've learned from my new life as a blogger is that there is nothing that people respond to more than writing that is raw, intimate, unfiltered. So that is the approach I took with this book. It was challenging at first, but ultimately very freeing. What's more, this approach ended up changing the way that I wrote the book. I actually posted parts of the book on the Huffington Post as I was working on them—and the feedback I got from people (often very personal and moving) proved invaluable. It shaped what I was writing and helped make the book what it eventually became.

Okay, my turn. I know I asked you before I did it, but when all was said and done, how did you feel about seeing aspects of your lives in the book?

ISABELLA: What made it all okay was that we saw your first draft and could change anything we wanted so that it reflected how we felt about those moments in our lives.

CHRISTINA: One of my favorite parts of the book is where you talk about how if we could TiVo our innermost thoughts we would see that not even our worst enemies talk about us the way we talk about ourselves. Do you still hear that inner critic?

ARIANNA: Look, it's an ongoing battle, and some days the inner critic—what I call the obnoxious roommate in our head—gets the upper hand. But by and large I have learned to turn down the volume and not listen. I've given my critical roomie an eviction notice . . . and when she does show up, I have learned that I can just walk out of the room.

CHRISTINA: What if she tries to follow you?

ARIANNA: Oh, she will . . . believe me! You just have to train yourself to stand up to her. And you do this by repetition. It's back to the idea that fearlessness is like a muscle. The more we refuse to buy into our inner critics—and our external ones too—the easier it will get to have confidence in our choices, and to feel comfortable with who we are.

ISABELLA: I know you've joked that your biggest fear is me getting my driver's license . . . but what would you say is really your biggest fear?

ARIANNA: My biggest fears revolve around the two of you—fear for your well-being, fear that I might be doing the wrong thing or making the wrong decision. There is nothing like becoming a mom to fill you with fear. I often think that when the doctors help take the baby out, they replace it with a combination of fear and guilt.

CHRISTINA: You make motherhood sound so appealing!

ARIANNA: I'm getting to the good part. . . . At the same time, there is nothing that can bring you closer to fearlessness about everything else in the world than being a parent—because everyday fears like not being approved of pale by comparison to the fears you have about your children.

What about you? What would say your biggest fears are?

CHRISTINA: My biggest fears come from the bad things in my head, but I know that when I say or think something bad about myself I have the power to put it aside and not let it determine my behavior—or even my feelings.

ISABELLA: My biggest fear is the fear of failing—the fear of trying something new and not being able to do it or not being good at it. I also have a fear of making the wrong choices when I'm young—which will have a negative impact later in my life.

CHRISTINA: Before, you asked us how we felt about having some of the more private parts of our lives talked about in the book . . . specifically some of the issues we've dealt with surrounding food. Given what you just said about your biggest fears being about us, did dealing with these kinds of things help you become more fearless or did it make you more afraid?

ARIANNA: Great question. It did both. When I saw what was going on first with Isabella and then later with you . . . it scared the living daylights out of me. But then, rather quickly, I got out of fear mode and into protective mother mode. I had to push the fear aside and take action. The need to help—to do something now—filled me with strength and a fearlessness that surprised even me.

Seeing you dealing with so many of the same fears I was burdened with made me want to figure out why this was, and what we could do to stop it. And, in the end, dealing with those issues was one of the main reasons I decided to write a book exploring fearlessness.

ISABELLA: Well, if you wrote this book for us, what is it that you'd most like Christina and me—and the other mothers and daughters out there—to take away from it?

ARIANNA: The single most important thing I hope you—and everyone else—take away is the notion that a fear-driven life is a life not fully lived. And that by living in fearlessness we can change ourselves and change the world for the better.

I'm convinced that the more fearless we are in our personal lives, the more of that spirit we'll bring to changing our world. And it desperately needs changing. Really, what's the point of being fearless if you're not going to use it to try and achieve big things?

All right, before we wrap this up, what do you think other mothers and daughters would get out of reading *On Becoming Fearless*?

CHRISTINA: I think it comes down to what you say in the book about how important it is to build a "fearless tribe"—surrounding ourselves with those people who will always be in our corner, always there for us, whether we succeed or fail. And hopefully that starts with those closest to us . . . mothers and daughters, sisters and cousins . . . and friends.

ISABELLA: I think discussing the ideas in the book will definitely help bring mothers and their daughters closer together. Seeing all the things they have in common—both good and bad—and figuring out together how to make the move from fear to fearlessness.

QUESTIONS AND TOPICS
FOR DISCUSSION

1. For the person in your group who chose *On Becoming Fearless,* what prompted this choice? If you were not the one who selected the book, are you pleased to have read it? Why or why not?

2. Arianna Huffington shares many personal stories and anecdotes in this book. Were you surprised at her level of honesty? Did learning about her struggles and triumphs change your view of how fearlessness can be achieved? How so?

3. Discuss the ways in which the media influence society's ideas about physical appearance, aging, motherhood, and professional development as it pertains to women.

4. Share one positive influence or role model, either from *On Becoming Fearless* or of your own choosing.

5. "Intelligent, smart, talented, hardworking women allow themselves to be lost in the quest for one man's approval," writes Huffington (page 43). Why is women's self-image so often tied in to what men—in many instances one particular man—think of them? Why do you suppose some women (even "fearless" ones) act weak in order to appear more attractive to men?

6. Huffington, the mother of two daughters, writes that in the modern era "all of our traditional fears about our children's safety and well-being are multiplied and magnified" (page 59). How is parenting in today's world different from what it was a generation ago? Do you find

it helpful to talk to other parents and share advice? What are some things parents can do to foster fearlessness in their children?

7. Each chapter begins with a different woman's story about fearlessness, from writer Nora Ephron to actress Diane Keaton to Kathy Eldon, a documentary producer whose photographer son was murdered by a mob in Somalia. In what ways did these stories add to the experience of reading this book? Which story affected you the most?

8. "There is a professional double standard so that the same behaviors that help men get ahead and prove their worth on the job are discouraged in women" (page 90). What are these double standards, and why do they persist? Do you agree with the author that the responsibility for double standards in the workplace lies with both men and women? How so?

9. Fearlessness in a sense starts with our physical well-being. "When we feel strong, when our bodies are healthy, we don't feel as vulnerable as when we are weak and out of shape," says Huffington. "It's harder to feel fearless when we become breathless climbing up a flight of stairs" (page 28). Has reading this book inspired you to improve your physical health as a step toward becoming fearless?

10. In some instances women are held back not only by their own self-censors but by the fear of society's censure, leading to "the primal fear of being shunned by the tribe" (page 47). How much influence does the fear of nonconformity have on women's decision making?

11. How important is it to have a fearless role model in one's life? What is your opinion of Huffington's mother, whom the author talks

about throughout the book? In what ways did she contribute to her daughter's fearlessness?

12. When you were a child, unaware of the idea of "fearlessness," were you naturally fearless? If so, what memories do you have of acting fearless as a child?

13. What is your overall impression of *On Becoming Fearless*? Of the areas explored in the book—body and looks, love, parenting, work, money, aging and illness, death, and leadership—which one resonated with you the most? Why?

14. Do you have a group of women whom you rely upon for support? Do these women make you fearless? Share stories of how these women have inspired you.

15. Did you come away with any concrete advice to apply to your own life after reading *On Becoming Fearless*? If so, share with the group what you'd most like to accomplish.

ARIANNA HUFFINGTON'S SUGGESTIONS
FOR FURTHER READING

Little Women by Louisa May Alcott

The Female Brain by Louann Brizendine, MD

Jane Eyre by Charlotte Brontë

Madame Bovary by Gustave Flaubert

The Second Stage by Betty Friedan

Mythology: Timeless Tales of Gods and Heroes by Edith Hamilton

The Scarlet Letter by Nathaniel Hawthorne

A Doll's House by Henrik Ibsen

To Kill a Mockingbird by Harper Lee

Reviving Ophelia: Saving the Selves of Adolescent Girls by Mary Pipher

The Tempest by William Shakespeare

The Joy Luck Club by Amy Tan

The Beauty Myth: How Images of Beauty Are Used Against Women by
Naomi Wolf

A Room of One's Own by Virginia Woolf

ARIANNA HUFFINGTON'S
TOP 10 TIPS
TO BECOMING FEARLESS

1. Be true to yourself. Constantly looking over your shoulder for approval means you'll never find it. What's more, you greatly increase your chances of walking into a wall or falling into a ditch — not to mention losing yourself in the process.

2. Turn down the volume of your inner critic. Everyone has one: the obnoxious roommate in your head, always there with the critical, self-doubting comment. But that doesn't mean you have to listen. When the negative judgments start to blare, hit the off switch or drown them out with your iPod.

3. Look past the glass ceiling to endless opportunity. Preoccupation with impediments allows us to climb only so high. Keep your mind open to new adventures and you'll surpass every expectation.

4. Use the mirror to make sure your lipstick isn't smudged, not to judge your value as a person.

5. Stop comparing yourself to others — it's a no-win game. And especially stop comparing yourself to supermodels, who don't even look like the perfectly lit and airbrushed supermodels we usually see in magazines.

6. Get enough sleep. It's next to impossible to be fearless — or to be your best self — if you are sleep deprived. A good pillow is a vital addition to any beauty regime.

7. Slip into an air of self-assurance. Fearlessness is sexy. So is confidence.

8. Run, swim, bike, hike, do yoga, or hit the gym. And fill your lungs with fresh air. Never forget—you can go weeks without food, days without water, but only mere minutes without breathing.

9. Be assertive in love. Know what you want out of a relationship and have the courage to express yourself to get it. And if you don't get it—and if the other person can't even handle the mere expression of your needs—be strong enough to walk away.

10. Always remember: True fearlessness comes from a deep and complete acceptance of ourselves—not from what we wear, or how we look, or what we do, or what we accomplish.